MEMORIES

Reubens School
1930-1970
An Anthology

MEMORIES

Reubens School

1930-1970

An Anthology

Text and images Copyright 2014 by the Individual Contributors

All Rights Reserved

Used here by permission

This Anthology Copyright 2014 Intermountain North Publishing

All Rights Reserved

About the Cover.
The photo on the front cover is undated, but obviously was taken when the building was unoccupied. That could have been after it was abandoned following consolidation in 1962 or before it was occupied in 1910. The presence of weeds growing through cracks in the wooden sidewalk, what look to be protective cages around newly planted trees and the fact the bell is still in the belfry point to an early date. We have chosen the summer of 1910 before the first classes started as the likely date of the photo.

DEDICATION

This book is dedicated to the memory of the students and teachers no longer with us who made our School and the Reubens community the great institutions they were, and to our friend and classmate, Howard Stolte, who recently passed away. He will be sorely missed at this year's Reunion since he and his wife Janette faithfully supported them for many years.

ACKNOWLEDGEMENTS

This book was born out of a desire to capture the delightful stories and history of the Reubens community and Reubens School. It could only have come about with the help of many individuals. Our thanks and appreciation to all who willingly gave of their time to make it possible!

Our initial plan in 2011 was to make a memory album of stories submitted to an Album Committee. However, since many expressed their desire to have copies, we then pursued the challenge of publishing these stories in a book. We here express our thanks to members of the reunion planning committee for supporting this effort; we felt free to proceed because of their interest and encouragement.

When we sought advice from the Ilo-Vollmer Historical Society in Craigmont we found them supportive and helpful, for which we are quite grateful. They encouraged us to publish these memories, for which we here express our heartfelt thanks.

With no experience in publishing books and feeling overwhelmed by the project, we presented the challenge at the 2013 Reubens All-School Reunion. Les and Donna Mae Huntley were present and Les volunteered his help. What a welcome offer! He has experience and expertise we lack. We are so grateful for his willingness to help us see this book published. Thank you, Les!

And our heartfelt thanks to all who submitted stories and photos; it has been a joy to read them. In sharing a portion of your lives with us you have helped preserve the memories of an interesting and by-gone era. Our thanks to all! Dorothy Scott helped us greatly by proof reading these pages. Thank you, Dorothy, you made this a much better book than it would otherwise have been.

And finally, we must never us forget that it was the close-knit Reubens community who supported us in all our school activities and the dedicated faculty and the ever-changing student body who made our school what it was and what we are. We have preserved these memories in your honor and hope you enjoy what you find here.

REUNION HISTORY

The first Reubens School reunion began with a phone call to classmates of the 1945 graduates some years ago. Telva Timmons Goffinet was the instigator and a tradition began. Attending that first gathering "for lunch", at the Helm Restaurant in Lewiston, along with Telva, were, Dean Huffman, Jack and Betty Curry, Bud and Maxine Chambers and Neva O'Brien. Each year, by "word of mouth" the gathering continued.

In 1997 the first recorded Reubens All School reunion was held at the Helm in Lewiston and has continued annually. Each year a majority vote determined if the next reunion would be in Lewiston or Reubens. The year 2000 found the fourth gathering in the Community Center in Reubens. There 140 graduates, teachers, students and spouses gathered to give congratulations and best wishes to two special graduates of the long-gone high school. Alice Russell Cannon 97, and Ruth Webb Scott 93, celebrated their 78th and 74th graduation anniversaries and were the oldest of the 49 graduates attending the reunion.

For 52 years the Reubens school graduated between one and 10 students. Their graduation pictures hang on the wall of the community Center displaying the hairstyles and clothes from bygone fashion. Memorabilia including school papers, annual yearbooks and trophies are displayed proudly in showcases.

Each reunion recognizes the graduating class celebrating its 50th anniversary and memorializes the students and teachers who have passed away during the preceding year. Through the years, volunteers have stepped forward to chair the event and plan the activities. As with the school, for years a large and stately high school, the reunion though enjoying strong support will eventually dwindle along with the population of graduates and become part of Reuben's history.

A DVD created to preserve the memories and history of the Reubens School, is available along with this "Memory Book" which is a collection of pictures and stories of students, activities and events as recalled by those who attended Reubens School.

CONTENTS

Introduction   15

A Brief History of Reubens   22

Class of 1933

Edith Webb Vannoy   25

Class of 1940

Mr. James Vannice   29

Byron Webb   31

Class of 1942

Maxine Webb Henerson   35

Class of 1943

Max Skelton   37

Class of 1944

Leonard O'Brien   41

Class of 1945

Telva Timmons Goffinet   45

Reubens School Memories

Dorothy Toomb Scott   47

Class of 1948

Bill Wood   53

Class of 1950

Birdie West   55

Everta Jeanne Leeper Thomason   57

Mildred Timme   61

Leona Becker Armstrong   62

Calista Arlene Brackett Moore   63

Gerrie Meier Johnson   63

Class of 1951

Nancy Teats Flint   65

Grace Moore Weinert   66

Class of 1952

Raydene Cannon Lowe   69

Joanne (Joan) Lewis   71

Laurine Skelton Nightingale   72

Howard Stolte   78

Frances L. West Holdorf   80

Rosie M. Meier Stellmon   84

Class of 1953

G. Arthur Misner, Jr.   87

Glen Cannon   89

Class of 1954

Don Moore   91

Class of 1955

Charlotte Ruckman Misner   93

Charlotte's Tribute to Leo Rieman   95

Donna Mae Leeper Huntley   98

Doran Rogers   103

Fred O'Brien   106

Class of 1956
Lawrence Courtney   111

Class of 1957
Larry L. Curry   113
Ronald Stellyes   114

Class of 1959
Ann Knowlton Curry   115
Loretta Skelton Stevens   116
Gary Willson   117
Patsy Symmes Gjendem   118

Class of 1960
Eileen Stauty Brackett   123
Dennis Decicio   124

Class of 1964
Janice Dau Taft   131

Class of 1966
Barbara Becker Kotz   133

Class of 1969
Jerene Behler Gertonson   135

Class of 1970
Janice Coon Hartig   137

PREFACE

I've called this collection of personal stories an "anthology" at first reluctantly for lack of a better word but now with enthusiasm having learned the Greeks used the word to describe "a collection of flowers". That word very well describes this collection of life stories, a mixed collection of wild flowers I have been privileged to read, edit and present to you.

There is wildness about many of the young people you will meet here, a wildness fitting for those who grew into adulthood in what was once a wilderness of towering pines filled with grazing wildlife. But their wildness was not just because of where they grew up, or maybe it was at that. They came into the world when people sometimes did wild things just for fun, calling them practical jokes and pulling them on others, often to "put them in their place" in a way that could be avenged only by another practical joke.

One such was pulled by a threesome of fathers of teens whose stories appear here. Donna Mae's dad, Vinal Leeper along with Fred's dad, Ray O'Brien and probably George Dau as well, exacted revenge on a local farmer who had done something they deemed worthy of avenging. The farmer had won a live goose in a raffle, and knowing he'd lose it unless he took good care of it, locked it in the trunk of his car.

He locked the trunk but not the car doors for in those days no one locked anything even at night. The conspirators slipped away from whatever festivities were underway, crawled into the unlocked car, removed the back seat then the goose and put everything back together again. The story goes that they took the goose to one of their homes, cooked it and ate it, no doubt with great relish. Given the times and the customs of the times, there can be no doubt the wives were involved in the prank right along with their husbands.

Most of those you will meet here grew up in waning years; WWII was over and home front difficulties were winding down. Motor vehicles were replacing horse and buggy, diesel trucks and good roads were stealing from the railroad the traffic that had lured it to the area. Consolidation had taken their school away and TV viewing was gnawing away at the neighborliness that once flourished in the small town. The social structure was falling apart.

Reading here the happy stories of times in school and the useful and productive lives that followed, you may sense a longing for a departed era, an era when neighbors visited neighbors, the coffee pot was always on, and no one even thought of locking doors at night. As you read these stories by young people grown into oldsters like those you meet everywhere today, remember when and where they came from and understand the look you see on their faces is one of longing for something, some time, they will never see again. Think of them as wildflowers in a place where they, like dandelions, are considered a nuisance, not as they, and dandelions, were and still can be a source of beauty, healing and other good things.

Editor

Note: I have removed birth and wedding dates throughout because such personal information is often used for passwords and security phrases.

INTRODUCTION

Les Huntley, Editor

This is a book of stories, stories about a small town at the brink of Lapwai Canyon in North Central Idaho told by those who lived there and attended school there. Some married there and raised their families there; few still live there for theirs are stories of life in a small town slowly dying from neglect. Some stories focus solely on the school years and others are more complete.

These are their stories, very much as we received them. Here you will get a glimpse into the lives of boys and girls shaped by that town, that community, and especially by their school. Give a smile and a mental handshake as you meet them and get to know them.

It would help, I am sure, to set the stage before going on. This town, this community, did not just appear out of nothing. Like everything else, it has its history. Here is a glimpse of the backstory for the town and people you will meet herein.

Before 1906 there was no town of Reubens, just a plot of ground midway between the villages of Chesley to the northwest, Lookout and Gifford to the north, Melrose to the northeast and Kippen to the south. Reubens, a railroad town, owes its existence to the railroad, it was built by the railroad, for the railroad. The railroad, the Northern Pacific, had finished its long meander down the Potlatch River through Kendrick and Juliaetta to where the Potlatch merges with the Clearwater. At Arrow Junction the railroad divided, its eastern branch heading upriver to Orofino, Kamiah and beyond and the western branch downriver to Lewiston, Idaho's only seaport and North Idaho's one city then worthy of being called a city.

Ten or so miles west of Arrow Junction, at the mouth of Lapwai Creek near the old town of Spaulding the railroad spurred off to the south following the creek east toward a fertile high plateau with its rich farmlands and abundant standing timber. There were fortunes to be made in hauling the produce of those lands down to the river for shipment to far away markets. And, all railroads, this one included, were focused on making money.

Reubens exists because the Northern Pacific thirsted for money and more money. It acquired some of that money by holding for ransom the towns through which the rail line might pass. If the citizens of the town agreed to supply the railroad with the land and money they demanded, the railroad would pass through or near the town. If they would not, the railroad would build a new town nearby bringing economic disaster to their town.

The prairies east and southeast of Reubens provide ample evidence of that practice. Present day Craigmont was blessed with a new town, Vollmer, when Ilo a little to the west refused to pony up. Not long after, the citizens of Ilo took their revenge by moving their town lock stock and barrel down beside Vollmer. Ferdinand, eight miles to the south also refused to cooperate and was "blessed" by a new town, Steunenberg, a short distance to the northeast. Ferdinand's ethnic German and strongly Catholic populace simply ignored the new town and left it to die on the vine.

Another eight miles south, the citizens of Cottonwood agreed to Northern Pacific's demands and the town survived and thrived. Eight or so miles east of Cottonwood, the booming town of Denver, established in hope of becoming a railroad town, was disappointed when the NP chose to build a new town, Fenn, some five miles to the south. In 1945 only a few occupied homes and the flour mill were scattered along Denver's once busy streets. In 2013 there remained nothing of Denver but plowed ground and the crumbling remains of its once flourishing flour mill.

Those are the conditions in which Reubens came into existence. In 1906, the year of Reubens; founding, there was a thriving little town, Kippen, at the crossroads about one mile south of the new Reubens town site. This writer does not know what deals may have been offered in the area; it is certain that there were no takers of any deals offered since Reubens was born, or rather, created.

As happened with Idaho's Denver, the small towns surrounding Reubens withered and died as commerce and population gravitated to the railroad for its quick, convenient and relatively inexpensive access to the outside world. Kippen to the south was one of them, as were Chesley, Lookout, Gifford and Melrose.

By late 1905 or early 1906, after a long, tough and very expensive climb of more than 2000 feet out of Lapwai Canyon, the railroad finally emerged from its last tunnel a short way northwest of Chesley. Bypassing that prosperous little town in making its way to Reubens, the NPRR assured Chesley's demise just as it had so many like it. Chesley would not have suited anyway since the railroad needed a town at the very top of that long climb.

Reubens was established in 1906 and the privilege of naming it fell to the uncle of a lady, Edith Webb Vannoy, whose story appears first in these Memories. As she tells it, her uncle, Emmette Webb, was a railroad employee involved in what went on in Reubens' birthing on the prairie atop that long climb from the Clearwater valley. When asked how he came up with that name, he said a man of the NezPerce tribe introduced himself as "Reuben. from Webb", no doubt referring to the Webb Store. Emmette was amused at the thought of introducing himself as "Webb from Reubens" and that's how the town got its name. You will find a different version of the story in the history immediately following this Introduction.

Reubens was an important stop on the railroad. It could not have operated its spur line across Camas Prairie without the Reubens rail yard. And there was where the extra engines needed to push and pull the trains up from the canyon floor were dropped off, and where they were picked up for the return trip to Lewiston, There

CPRR Depot, Reubens, Idaho

too the locomotives were watered and refueled for their trek across Camas Prairie to Grangeville at the end of the line.

Reubens was a railroad town but refused to be just another railroad town. It became the center of a tight knit community of townspeople, farmers and ranchers, just as did so many small towns of the day. And, just as elsewhere, that community orbited around the people who lived there, loved there, raised families there. One focus of the Reubens community was the Presbyterian Church dedicated in 1906 about the time the town was birthed. Another focus was the new school, built in 1908 to educate the children of the town and nearby farms.

Reubens Presbyterian Church building is still standing more than 100 years later. A few years ago, Presbyterians tired of supporting a small church in a dying town and too poor to pay its pastor, abandoned it. One of the men brought up in the community, educated in the school and shaped by the Church, Dennis Decicio, whose story appears in these Memories, pastors the small congregation of what is now Reubens Community Church as this is written.

Reubens First Presbyterian Church

Yes, the town is dying, as railroad towns always die when their railroad dies. Reubens' railroad, now Camas Prairie Rail Road, began to shrivel in the 1950s when cars and trucks and the gasoline to fuel them became plentiful and reasonably priced at the end of WWII. These, coupled with roads again kept in good repair, made it easy for shoppers and shippers to travel by highway to Lewiston and its shopping and shipping points.

Soon the steam driven passenger and mail service was replaced with what some on Camas Prairie called the "Galloping Goose" but Reubens knew as the "Bug", a two car, noisy, diesel-driven, smelly and increasingly little–used substitute. Eventually that stopgap saw its own demise as diesel powered trucks and family autos took away its business. Yes, the railroad was dying, and along with it the town.

The town had suffered major problems of its own over the years. First the economic problems of the Great Depression devastated Reubens' business community. As you will read herein, some of the highly respected businessmen were forced into bootlegging to feed and clothe their families.

At least three huge fires, the last of which in 1955 destroyed almost all the businesses still operating there, devastated the town. When Donna Mae and I were living north of town in the 1970s, there were only a few businesses still operating. Among them were Frank West's garage, Vince and May Sanders' Wayside Inn, the Thomason Chemical Company operated by Bill Thomason and his brothers, the Lewiston Grain Growers elevators and a post office operating out of a family residence. The Presbyterian Church maintained a fair sized congregation, and schoolchildren were bussed to Craigmont.

Yes, the town was dying and still is. But, odd as it may seem, the Community still continues its vigorous existence. The heart of any organization, towns included, is its community. Here the community was and still is held together by several things. First, is the people themselves, people who tell some of their stories here. Good, hardworking, honest and God fearing people can't be kept from coming together to form a good hardworking and God fearing Community.

Next in importance was the school, built in 1908 and occupied continuously from its opening in 1910 until consolidation closed its doors in 1962. The lives of good people are centered on their children; their children are involved with school, so the parents are also. Of slightly less importance because not supported by everyone, was the Church. Good churches inevitably become centers for good communities.

First Graduating Class - 1914
Caroline Curtiss Wallace Scott Caroline Nichol

Then there were the clubs: the Garden Club and the Community Club. Here is where the heart of any community, the wives, mothers and grandmothers met to share their lives and plot their projects. Those ladies' projects don't necessarily determine the health of the community, but they certainly impact its flavor, its heart, the things that make it uniquely *that* community.

Now you'd think losing your school, then the heart of the town by fire, and a fair share of the population leaving the farms to find easier, better paying jobs elsewhere would devastate a community. Not so the Reubens community! It simply recognized and accepted the new reality, adapted to it and went right on doing pretty much what it had always done. The State deeded the abandoned gym to the town, which converted it into a Community Center and formed a taxing district to fund its operations. The Community Club claimed and still operates the kitchen because they had equipped and supplied it.

In 1964 the Church needed to raise money to fund a new roof for the church building. Bill Thomason and others decided to host a sausage feed using the Community Center kitchen and dining areas. The sausage feed was such a success it was repeated the next year and every year since. This is a community project raising funds for community needs. It thrives today because community members who have moved away still trek back to Reubens the first Sunday in March to help with *their* sausage feed.

Yes, the Reubens Community still carries on, though the town is a shadow of its old self. The annual reunion of former schoolmates that inspired the production of this book plays a large part in that carrying on. But I must end this introduction with the sad recognition that even these reunions will not carry on forever.

The ones who attend these reunions, those shaped by the school, the church and the community are fewer each year. Their children and grandchildren are now far away and most have never really been part of the community.

Eventually this great community will come to an end, and it is partly for that reason we publish this Memory Book. It is our fervent hope that reading the stories of those who attended this great old school and weathered the economic and other storms endured by our community, will somehow strengthen and encourage its readers as they together form and shape new, unique, communities of their own.

A Brief History of Reubens

Submitted by Laurine Nightingale

At the time of the opening of the Reservation there were two main roads leading to the NezPerce Prairie. The first road skirted the western boundary of the Reservation enroute from Lewiston to Mt. Idaho. The second road was the one long used by Indians as a means to travel southward from the Clearwater River via Lapwai Creek through the forest at the top of the grade. The present NezPerce County road from Culdesac to Reubens follows this route.

The opening of the Reservation found many homesteaders eager to file a claim; among the first in the Reubens country were David Kippen and his wife, Ida, who took up the land adjacent to land that contained the famous Cold Spring. Opening the Reservation created a great demand for lumber. To meet this need Mr. Erickson in 1897 moved a mill to an area about one mile southeast of where the depot would be located. A town sprang up around the mill and a store and a school were established.

The Northern Pacific Railroad announced the construction of a railroad through Culdesac to the Camas Prairie. This brought about a flurry of excitement within Kippen. New hotels and livery barns were constructed while homemakers prepared to take in boarders. In the spring of 1906 two hundred men were working on five camps to house N.P.R.R. construction workers between Culdesac and Kippen. They constructed a long "Y" for turning the engines at the top of the hill and the sidetracks needed around the depot.

While the Erickson Mill at Kippen was the only sawmill in the area, the "boom" at Kippen was short lived; the depot would not be placed at Kippen but at Reubens. Many people felt that shrewd financial and business deals led the railroad to establish its depot near the "Y", while others felt that the location near the "Y" was selected because it was nearer the three then thriving towns of Melrose, Lookout and Gifford, each of which was in a highly productive area. During the winter of 1905-1906, George, Pete and Martin Pankey felled the trees on the town site and the other trees that later formed the timber for the railroad tunnels.

View From the Water Tower, Undated

After the Fire, 1955

Reubens was named after an Indian known as Reuben. Reuben came into Emmett Webb's store and asked why the store was called Webb's Store; since it was on Reuben's land it should be called Reuben's Store. When the question of a suitable name for the town arose, Mr. Webb related his encounter with the Indian Reuben and it was agreed that this was reason enough to call the town Reubens.

After the town site had been laid out, George O. Farr became agent for the town site in 1906. The first residence was that of Mr. and Mrs. F.E. Erickson, now owned by Steve Hill, This was the birthplace of the first child born in Reubens, Edna Marie Erickson. She was born October 31, 1906, and died January 25, 1907. She was also the first one to die in Reubens.

The first businesses were the Heck Hotel, Ford's Meat Market and a General store operated by Art Skelton. Later followed a Hardware Store, the Bank of Reubens, Erickson Hotel, a newspaper called the "Reuben News Era", a Livery Barn, Barber Shop and a Blacksmith Shop. H. L. Brown established a Drug Store in the same building with the Post Office and ran it for many years.

By becoming a major grain shipping point, Reubens proved the faith held by the Railroad. Grain from Gifford, Melrose and Lookout came to Reubens to the Kerr Gifford, Vollmer Clearwater Grain Company and Tri-State Bal Four Guthrie Warehouses. The School was built halfway between Kippen and Reubens, for at that time there were more children from Kippen than Reubens.

Class of 1933

Edith Webb Vannoy

Spouse: Allie (Al) Vannoy

[Fred O'Brien's tribute to his aunt Edith at the 2013 Reunion]

Edith Webb Vannoy was born September 30, 1915 to Ernest and Lula Webb.

She grew up in the Reubens, Craigmont area, (her family moved to Craigmont in 1929) graduating from Craigmont High School in 1933, 80 years ago. We still claim her as a Reubenite however.

Edith always said she would never marry a farmer. But then -she met Allie and his new car. Allie must have really twanged her heart strings as she wound up giving the ring back to this other feller. Allie said he wasn't sure which caused this happy event the new car or his good looks.

Allie says that he believes that the reason that she did not want to marry a farmer was that she had stayed with Ray and Marie O'Brien when she was little and watched Marie (her sister and my mom) slop the hogs. Well, as things happen, she ended up slopping the hogs on her own farm. As a young farm wife, she had to go through the bull pen to slop the hogs. They were raising a bull calf for meat and the calf found out that she was afraid of him and the calf would chase her every time she went out to feed the hogs.

My mother always called Edith and Allie the "kids". Even when mom was 90 years old she would say, "I wonder what the kids are doing." Edith would have been 78 years old at that time. I guess that some people never grow old.

I left my mark on Edith's life. Well, maybe not her life, but certainly on her walls. When I was a small child I used crayons to decorate the walls in her beautiful new home. I still remember the incident because of the impression that my mother made on me.

I don't know why she worried about what I did to Edith's house because Edith was harder on it than I was. She was working with Uncle Allie driving the tractor while he ran the slip leveling the dirt around the new construction. Somehow she managed to run the tractor into the house, punching a hole in the house and breaking the crank off of the tractor. Allie said that she never drove the tractor again after that.

Edith's parents had friends who lived at Toppenish, Washington. They visited them every summer. Because their only child, "Alice Tafferine", as she called herself, was about the same age as Edith, they invited Edith to go home with them. Edith says that she went because she had never been farther than Lewiston and Toppenish seemed a long way away. Alice Tafferine didn't know how to play. Edith had played with her sister Eupha who had a great imagination. Edith says that they could make paper dolls tell a good story.

Edith soon grew homesick and wanted to go home. She was glad when the father of Alice Tafferine said he had some business in Lewiston and would take her home. Then he started doing strange things to his old touring car, taking out the back seats and placing gallon jugs on the floor. Then he covered them with a long board and his wife laid blankets over the board. He informed the girls that the jugs were filled with water to put in the radiator in case the old car got hot. But Edith was no dummy; she had seen jugs like that before. In fact she was a bootlegger's daughter.

 Alice's father told them both to sit on the board and play with their dolls, especially if anyone stopped the car. No one stopped the car and they finally got to Lewiston after a most uncomfortable trip. She wasn't very old but she was scared of the Revenuers.

During those years, many families became bootleggers in order to survive. Later on Edith had the opportunity to ride shotgun for her sister Eupha running bootleg booze on the Camas prairie for her father. What a wild young woman she must have been.

We love you Aunt Edith. Happy 80th anniversary of your graduation from high school.

POSTSCRIPT: Edith and Allie retired from farming and moved to Lewiston about 12 years ago, where they have stayed in touch with old friends and made many new ones. Allie was always a good story teller, and Edith had typed many of them up for him. In the summer of 2012, they let themselves be talked into publishing their book, *"A Nice Car, A Good Woman -A Little Fun Every Day"*.

Their book was a local hit, selling 150 or so in the local market and maybe as many as 250 total. Published on Amazon, sales still trickle in at one or two a month. I don't know how many Al gave away, but it must be close to a hundred. Quite an accomplishment for a 100 year old man and his 96 year old wife.

Booksigning July, 2012

With Byron Webb, 2013 Reunion

This couple is one of the great ones that just keep on keeping on, always looking for the bright side and mostly enjoying a little fun every day. As this is written, though, that has been tough to do, since Al has had a string of setbacks involving diagnoses and treatment for cancer, broken bones and a general loss of strength that tries hard to steal his joy but hasn't quite been able to do that. Edith has suffered almost as much as Al, sticking by him as he endured the pain and dealt with far too many side problems.

Loving care by their faithful sons Don and Stan and their families, along with extraordinary care by doctors, nurses and other caregivers seem to have helped Al turn the corner toward renewed health and vigor. Pain is largely controlled, side problems are still an issue, but the future looks brighter. Most important of all, both Al and Edith know where they are going when they leave this life. That is a blessing to them and a great blessing to those who love them.

CLASS OF 1940

Mr James Vannice

My time as a student at Reubens was short but memorable. We arrived at Reubens in the fall of 1934 and I started school as a 7th grader. I completed 3 years before we left the area and I continued my education in 2 other school systems before graduating High School in 1940 at Westport, Oregon.

While at Reubens, we lived at the ranch just west and over the tracks from the school. The house still stands and is on the property where the water column is situated. We farmed that ranch plus 2 other places, all with horses.

My vision of those few short years is memorable. Visions of the steam locomotive making its daily trek from Lewiston to Grangeville and back remain implanted in my mind. The winters were severe. No 4-wheel-drive vehicles or snow-removal-equipment for the roads. Our only transportation to the outside world was by the daily train.

Winter recreation consisted of sledding, skiing, bonfires and marshmallow roasts. Spring brought energy and new life to the area. One of our favorite pastimes was to pack lunches and head for the canyon to explore the tunnels and trestles, and to throw rocks at the insulators on the poles. Most of the summer was spent farming and putting up the winter supply of hay. I don't have the slightest idea of how many tons of dust I inhaled while following a team of horses harrowing summer fallow. I sharpened my eye with a 22 shooting squirrels. There was a bounty on squirrel tails and I turned in enough to buy my ammunition

I have returned to Reubens on more than one occasion and find the loss of landmarks depressing. I remember well the two mercantile stores. One was owned by the Webb family. Then there were the two grain elevators, the tavern and pool hall owned by a family by the name of Zilliox (sp), the drug store, post office, automotive garage, gas pump and creamery.

I can't forget the gymnasium and the icy cold shower rooms The old school house is gone The Church remains in the same location. Many houses are gone and some have been upgraded. The old wooden water tower is gone.

A few family names remain as memories. Mrs. Ruckman, a teacher who was a strict disciplinarian. There were 3 Ruckman girls, Virginia, Kit and Ann. Believe Ann to be the only one remaining. Barney Webb

Old Reubens School Sold For Salvage, Brings $25

REUBENS — The old Reubens school, built in 1908 and vacant since 1964, has been sold for $25 to Jack Nightingale of Reubens for salvage, according to Robert C. Strom, school district board clerk at Craigmont.

The four-room building cost $7,000 to build in 1908. Four additional rooms were built on the rear of the school in 1932 and the structure was used until consolidation took high school students to Craigmont. The grade school was moved into a newly constructed gymnasium adjacent to the school.

Wallace J. Scott, who lives across the street from the school, was valedictorian of the first high school class to graduate from the school in 1914. He is the only survivor of that class. Other graduates were Catherine Nicol, Frank Surplus and Kathryn Curtiss.

Scott was born in Minnesota and came to Reubens with his family when he was 10, completing grade and high school here. He recalls an ancient tree nearby with a hangman's rope grown into the branches. According to an old story, some horse thieves were hanged in the tree, the last to achieve such notoriety in the vicinity.

In 1910, the two upper rooms of the school were used for high school students when seven were enrolled. Some were added during the four years, Scott said, and some moved away, leaving only four to graduate.

There were no school buses then, Scott recalled, and students got to school by foot or horseback from the four outlying districts of Melrose, Gifford, Lookout and Chesley. First teacher and high school principal was Mary Scherzer. Grade school principal in 1910 was E. N. Clark.

The 73 students enrolled in 1910 were divided into primary for the first six grades, intermediate for grades seven and eight and high school. An old newspaper account of the school opening also mentions a "principal's room" as a division, but Scott said that was likely a high school division.

Dismantling of the building will begin immediately.

WALLACE J. SCOTT

Lewiston Tribune March 9, 1967

was probably my closest friend. The Gillette family lived in the train depot. Mr. Gillette was the station master and there were two boys, Doran who was my age and Bobby. Wesley Markham was diabetic and a good friend.

First High School Graduating Class 1914

I remember Jim Skelton whose father ran one of the grain elevators. A family named Denny lived in the shadows of the old water tower. There were several families by the name of Scott.

I retired from the Navy in 1971 after having served for 30 years. My years saw me through WWII, Korea and Viet Nam up until my retirement. I live in Oak Harbor, Washington which is the home for the Navy's electronic warfare and maritime patrol squadrons.

I have two children, 3 grandchildren and 3 great grandchildren. I lost my first wife in 2002 and remarried in 2007.

Byron Webb

Memories? Heck, I can't remember what I had for lunch today.

I guess the most memorable thing I experienced was the bop on the head by Helen Ruckman. As I told her in later years, I don't remember what I did to receive the book to the head side. And I wish I knew because I sure as hell would never do it again. She was not only my favorite teacher, but also one of my favorite women of all time.

I told her daughter Kit about it some years later (just before she died from cancer) and she loved it. Kit was my classmate from grades one through seven, the last year Helen taught in Reubens.

Helen Ruckman was my seventh grade teacher, and what a great teacher she was! A bit sneaky she was in that she had her desk in the back of the room instead of the front as most teachers did. That let her see what mischief was going on and made it more difficult for us mischief-makers. "Of course I didn't know it then but I was just a dumb seventh grader".

But we had to try, and one day I was minding someone else's business instead of my own, and she "snuck" up on me with book in hand and laid it along-side of my head with some dispatch. Made my ears ring. Well, it was our misfortune that Mrs. Ruckman left Reubens to be near her husband who had a business in Moscow.

Byron with Al and Edie Vannoy 2006 Reunion

So fast-forward a few years through High School, World War II and a few years later when I decided to go back to college at the U of I. I was downtown one day and dropped in on Helen's husband Val just to say Hello and came out with a part time job. Which came in handy because I by that time had a wife and two kids, and the $200 a month I got from the GI bill did not fully support them.

Helen came into the store one day, and to remind her of the bop on the head, I kind of hid behind the counter and asked her, "You aren't carrying a book are you?" Right away she remembered what I was referring to and we had a good laugh. I told her I wondered if she did some damage to my brain. She assured me she could not tell any difference —like she thought I wasn't the brightest bulb in the chandelier to begin with.

But how I loved that lady! Helen was not only my favorite teacher but also she and Val were two of my favorite people of all time.

Another memorable thing is this: The Craigmont basketball team came to our gym late in the 1940 season unbeaten. We'd been drubbed in the games we'd played but we vowed this game would be different. We never had enough warm bodies to have a full floor scrimmage, but we did pretty well with what we had.

We had worked on stopping their plays in practice, and I can't remember being so "pumped", then or since, for a game of any kind. We "felt it", and we stopped them throughout the entire game. What a feeling! No handshakes after the game either.

They were not happy campers but we sure were. It made a successful season for us. As I recall, their team won the state Championship a year or two later, possibly the next year, as the team we beat were mostly juniors or younger. As best I can recall my teammates were Raymond and Robert Denny, Dwight Scott, Earl and Dean Simpson, and maybe another one or two.

Ah, and there is my oldest brother, Lee, one who took life as un-seriously as anyone I ever knew. He was called to Principal Milligan's office for some unknown infraction. Mr. Milligan had had Mr. Marquam fashion a wooden paddle to be used for disciplinary purposes and Bro Lee was his first client. He asked Lee to bend over and grab his ankles. Which he did, except instead of grabbing his own ankles, he grabbed those of Mr. Milligan, sat him on his backside then sat on him.

All in fun for him but taken rather seriously by others, notably my Dad, who was on the school board. To his credit, Mr. Milligan came to Lee's rescue and said the punishment might have been too harsh. So Lee got off without any serious penalties.

All six of the progeny of Charles and Annie Webb were graduates of Reubens High; Virginia in 1930, Lee in 1931, George in 1933, Dorothy in 1937, Claude in 1938, and of course, I in 1940.

CLASS OF 1942

Maxine Webb Henderson

Spouse: Wynne B. Henderson

I transferred to Reubens from Chaney Country School in the 5th grade. Mother drove to the 4 corners where I rode on to school with H.S. neighbors and moved to town when the roads were bad. Dad stayed home to care for cattle. I drove Carolyn and myself through High School and after graduation the school bus program began.

One school memory that entered my mind was the day in chemistry lab when our experiment suddenly flamed. My partner, Clifford Zolber, said, "Maxine, open the window," and dumped it from the second story.

I am grateful for life long friendships and happy memories.

CLASS OF 1943

Max Skelton

Spouse: Barbara Choate Skelton

I attended the Reubens school for 12 years. For my first second and third grade, my teacher was Mrs. Blakeman. When I was in the third grade my brother Norman was in the first. The train ran a short distance from the school and always blew the whistle at the railroad crossing. One day upon hearing the whistle, my brother jumped up and ran to the window and announced "there goes that God damn train." The teacher returned him to his seat and reprimanded him properly.

In the 4th-5th grade Mrs. Greer was my teacher, Cappie Laufer was my sixth grade teacher. She later married Earl Willson and remained in the Reubens community for the rest of her life.

Seventh and eighth grade teacher was Arthur Weberling. There were several teachers throughout high school. Marvin Baker was Superintendent when I was in grade 9 and 10. My Junior and Senior year Delmer Engelking was the Superintendent

During the summer between my junior and senior year, there was a program where the government would give money for student help. Bill Marquam, the janitor and shop teacher, came to me and asked if I would help him paint the outside of the schoolhouse during the summer time. It was a two story school so

CLASS OF 1943

MAX SKELTON

WESLEY MARQUAM

he had constructed a mechanism fixed up with two big hooks that went up into the shingles and a rope that came down over the side of the building securing the work platform that we would stand on. It was connected to an electric motor with a tork to raise and lower it. We could cover a sixteen foot section at a time.

We would start at the top under the edge of the roof and scrape the boards as we came down, then start back up and paint it. Then we would move over to the next sixteen feet and do the next section. About the second trip down, the rope on my side broke and let Bill, the paint and everything slide down covering me.

We finally got back down. It wasn't too bad though, we got it cleaned up and fixed the rope and finished the job. Bill Marquam would never say a cuss word in his life. His reply was "darn you Bill Marquam."

One memory is the day something hit me in the back of the head as I was leaving study hall. It was a piece of chalk launched by Bud Chambers. I picked it up and threw it back just as someone behind me picked me up off the floor and held me thinking I was the person who instigated all the trouble. It was Mr. Engleking. I didn't say anything. He looked at me quite serious and from then on wondered if I might be a trouble maker.

All my siblings Norman, Frances and Robert, went through school and graduated from Reubens except Norman who dropped out during high school. Norman was drafted into the Navy during the war but had a heart condition so returned home to help on the farm. He was an excellent mechanic. He passed away in 2007.

Frances married Bill Hallen and now lives in Lewiston. Robert served in the Air Corps during the Korean War as a airplane mechanic. After discharge he returned to the farm where he was using a cutting torch on a piece of iron that was laying across an empty oil barrel. Petroleum fumes in the barrel ignited. The explosion killed Robert. That was November 13, 1956.

I liked basketball but was not very good at it. We had a school orchestra that I played in. The teacher was Dale R. Code who also taught Grades, 4,5 and-6. He was drafted into the war and died while serving his country. He was a fine person and musician.

Wesley Marquam and I were the two Seniors in the Class of 1943. Russell Cannon had been a class mate for several years. War time jobs sent his family to Casper Wyoming when he was a Junior, leaving the two of us.

Wesley was four years ahead of me in school but suffered from severe diabetes and had to drop out of school. I caught up with him in our senior year. He was a very good photographer and photographed many school activities. For the Graduation exercise, we decided as Valedictorian and Salutatorian, it would be too much to memorize a speech and we would just read from notes we had written.

Mrs. Engelking had come in and wanted to listen to our speeches. We told her we were just going to read them rather than memorize them. She said "You are not going to read anything; you are going to memorize your speeches." This was the day before graduation. Wes and I went to the Engelking home and spent most of the night memorizing until Mrs. Engleking was satisfied we knew our speeches by heart.

After graduation I joined the Navy and spent a few years on a destroyer during the war. During this time my folks moved from Reubens to a little farm between Melrose and Gifford. When I was discharged I never lived in Reubens again.

When I first came back from the service, I worked for a friend who had a trucking business in Pomeroy. When the Korean War broke out, I was called back into service. After completing my military obligations, I worked for

Howard and Halleck sawmill in Winchester that had been purchased from Craig Mountain Lumber Company. Then I went to work for Potlatch in the paper mill in Lewiston as a machinist.

In 1959 I married Barbara Choate, the mother of two small girls who I raised as my own. In 1969 Potlatch built a sawmill in Western Samoa. I was sent there as a maintenance supervisor and spent four years in that country. Barbara and daughter Chris joined me there. Chris and two classmates received their education through the University of Phoenix. Later two grandchildren spent a year and half with us in Samoa.

Barbara passed away from cancer in 2008.

Samoa was a very primitive country. They were good people but their history was such that they did things differently than we did. A few older ones would go to New Zealand for schooling. A couple of the men learned English and I got one of them, Isa Sua, who was a machinist and was a very good worker, to come work for me in the mill .

He came over to visit after I returned to Lewiston. A good machinist in the valley offered him a job at another shop where he stayed a few years then returned to Samoa.

I retired from Potlatch in 1992 and continue to live in Lewiston.

Class of 1944

Leonard O'Brien

Spouses: Lenora O'Brien; Barbara O'Brien

Leonard, 1944

I started the 8th grade at Baker, a one-room school where I was the only kid in my grade from 1st through 7th. My folks decided to send me to school at Reubens about a month after I started 8th grade at Baker. I was very nervous at first, because I was sure that I would be far behind the rest of the class. But thankfully, that wasn't the case. I continued at Reubens until graduating in 1944.

The Baker School had a barn, two outhouses, a woodshed, cisterns, two big trees and several small ones. We used to play Blackman, Andy Over, Hide and Seek, Tag, Follow the Leader and Fox and Geese. We would coast down the hill when the snow was right.

When I was in first grade, my teacher had me draw a picture of a car. But being the artist I am not, I held up the picture up and said it looked more like a spud. That just fractured everybody in school and they all laughed. Of course, I think they poured it on a little extra because they could get away with it.

Loren and Duane Crow
Leonard O'Brien

I remember in the first grade how big those kids in the eighth grade looked sitting on the other side. I remember the programs we used to have at night and how different the school building looked when I was used to seeing it during the day. At night, they had kerosene lanterns burning and everything was changed. It was always fun. I remember the spelling bees too and wasn't much of a speller so I got out of that.

When I was in third grade the depression was going full blast, or it was still on anyway. Somehow the folks got new clothes for my sister and me. That morning when I started out to school I walked out of the house with these new clothes on and there were a lot of chickens in the yard. For some reason the chickens went squawking off across the yard, you know just like something was after them. I turned around and hollered at Mom, "Well even the chickens don't know me!"

And I'm glad I said that because that really let my mother know how much I appreciated the new clothes. She used to tell me about that story every once in a while. My first day at the new school in Reubens was an experience I'll never forget. The day before, my cousin called me a Swede and we got into a fight. He blacked my eye and I sent him home crying.

The next day I started the eighth grade in Reubens and the 7th and 8th grade boys decided to find out how tough I really was. I had a piece of paper in my hand that they thought they should have. I remember thinking that I'd let them kill me before I would let them have it. I never had any trouble with anybody the rest of my school years.

We had a makeshift baseball diamond behind the school that lacked about 100 feet of having enough outfield. I was in the outfield when Raymond Denney hit a ball way over my head and out into the road then rolled about 400 feet down the road. That's when I lost interest in baseball.

In my junior year, we had a dance to raise money. For some reason we didn't collect the money for tickets at the door but sold thickets during the dance. I asked a sailor to buy a ticket, not knowing armed forces need not pay. He didn't say anything, just took a roundhouse swing at me. He hit my sports coat and tore a button off. Two young men, Lee and George Webb, seeing what happened picked him up and heaved him out into the graveled street. All my life it has bothered me that I asked him for money.

Some other memories I have of Reubens School are walking part of the way on a wooden sidewalk to the gym which was a quarter mile away on Main Street. The old gym was either made out of an old dance hall, or a garage, I can't remember which. It had a wood stove in one back corner that didn't do much to heat the front of the gym in the winter. It had a cable bar across the center of the court that made long-range basketball shots nearly impossible.

The gym had a restroom for women and showers for both girls and boys that just drained out onto the ground. While I was in high school, they added a kitchen to one side of the gym

I graduated in 1944 and that summer was drafted into the Army. After basic training, I served in the Philippines and Japan until 1946 then returned home to work on the family farm. I continued farming there until I retired in 1985. I must have been doing something right because the NezPerce Soil and Water Conservation District named me Outstanding Supervisor from 1967-1974 and Farmer of the Year in 1984.

Lenora Rice and I were married in 1950, and were married for fifty years until her death in 2001. We moved to Lewiston when I retired and joined the Retired Teachers of North Idaho, where I continued my membership after Lenora's death even though I had never actually been a teacher.

Barbara and I were married in 2003. We continue to live in Lewiston, and enjoy travelling. Our favorite trips have been to Ireland, a cruise through the Panama Canal and a cruise to South America and "around the Horn". I still help out wherever I can, volunteering at the First Methodist Church, the Lewiston Veterans Home and at the Civic Theatre. And, I enjoy playing golf whenever possible.

Home from National Honor Flight
October, 2013

Seven Canyons, Sedona, Arizona

Class of 1945

Telva Timmons Goffinet

Spouse: Eldon Goffinet

My grade school years were spent at Melrose then my freshman and sophomore years were at Gifford. One of my teachers was John Tierney. He was a great educator and later married a Reuben's girl, Sylvia Kirkpatrick who was also teaching at Gifford. Sylvia was an R.H.S. graduate with the class of 1938.

When I came to Reubens my junior year the class consisted of Bud Chambers, Maxine Stellyes, Betty Chambers, Mary Palmer, Dean Huffman and myself. At mid term our senior year, we were joined by three junior class members, Elvin Simmons, Neva O'Brien and Louis Horvath. Neva and Elvin became Valedictorian and Salutatorian respectively.

We rode the bus to school, that was a Chevrolet delivery van. Herman Stellyes had the bus contract, but Bud Chambers drove it most of the time which probably was very illegal as he was one of the students.

Along with myself, students riding the bus were Jack Curry, Louis Horvath, Jackie, Gerrie and Rosie Meier, Sherel Tyler, Earl and Laura Tiede, Jean and Don Curry, the Brackett's, Arlene, Rena, Chuck and Jim, Maxine Stellyes and Lavon Chambers, and for awhile Delbert Kole.

We were "Sardine Packed".

Several of the students were couples back then, Bud and Maxine, Lavon and John Mehl, Leonard and Margaret Owens, Jack and Betty, Loren and Jackie.

Often during noon hour Jean and I would play the phonograph in the study hall and we would dance.

Our principal was an old religious nut and didn't like the popular song "Pistol Packing Mamma". He paid Louis two dollars to break the record. So I took my record to school. It didn't get broke.

This was during wartime and the students were asked to participate in selling war bonds. Jackie and I had some competition going as to who could raise the most money by auctioning bonds. Her dad, Art Meier and Fred Thomas were bidding against each other when Fred cast a bid of $8,000, the total profit from his crop of White Dutch Clover that year. Thus, declaring me the winner.

Our teachers were Mr. Shawen, Shirley Laird, Velma Scott (Denney), Barbara Sherwin (Hill).

One of the grade school teachers, Barbara Mjelde, was very artistic so we made paper mache figures of Flamingo Dancers and a Donkey for our Senior Prom that had a Spanish theme. We hired a five-piece band from Lewiston called Ray Mallory, a top band at that time. I believe we paid them $150 or $200 for the evening and had a full house.

The event was almost cancelled as that was the day President Roosevelt died and some thought we were disrespectful to hold the event.

In my younger years, my sister had a friend who played the piano, guitar and saw, which was quite an accomplishment in itself. I would listen to him play and then practice whistling the tune. I could imitate it very well. I was asked to perform for many occasions and continued until my sons were at the age of being embarrassed by my talent, so I retired it.

September after graduation I married Eldon Goffinet and we were married 37 years when he passed away. We raised two sons, Rocky and Ray.

I still live on the land my grandparents, Mary and William Timmons, homesteaded in 1895 and where I was born. Four generations of my family have spent their lives on this place near the old town site of Melrose.

At this writing there are four remaining graduates of the class of '45 enjoying what each day has to offer.

REUBENS SCHOOL MEMORIES 1946 – 1950
Dorothy Toomb Scott

I moved to Clarkston, Washington from eastern Oregon in the summer of 1946 to live with my grandparents and go to school at LCSC. I discovered that if I took a class in Idaho history and Idaho School Finance I could get a Provisional Teaching Certificate in the State of Idaho. I had a year of college to my credit and was hoping to continue my desire to be a teacher when college resumed in the fall but after finding out I could get a Provisional Certificate I enrolled in summer classes to take the two courses needed to comply. Those completed, I found three job openings I could qualify for and proceeded to investigate. One was in Genesee (too many relatives there that knew I was only 19 years old). One in Caldwell down south, where I was not interested in going, and one in Reubens.

I applied for the Reubens job and was called for an interview early in August. It was probably the hottest day of the summer the day my Aunt took me for the interview. Her car overheated and boiled going up the steep grade out of Culdesac. My aunt elected to walk to the closest house and get some water. (She wanted me to stay with the car). In the mean time, a pickup came along and offered to push the car up the remainder of the hill to get water. I said OK and we met her up there, got water and drove on to Reubens.

I met with Frank Symmes, the clerk of the school board, viewed the school and was offered the job. I met with the woman, Rose Scott, who provided room and board for single teachers and arranged to live with her and her husband Wallace. She had a lot of rules to abide by but I agreed to them. I could not use Kleenex in her home, I could only wash my hair on a designated day of the week, I could only wash out my hose in the bathroom sink, etc, etc. The thing that bothered me most was she kept asking me if I thought I was old enough to teach high school and control the students. From the time I moved in with her until the time I rented a house there in town with another teacher, she kept bugging me about my age and my ability to teach.

It was a wonderful year. In September of 1946, I met 21 anxious students (14 girls and 7 boys). They and their parents accepted me warmly and I formed many new friends that very first year. However, at the first PTA meeting the MC asked everyone in attendance who had been a former teacher at Reubens to please stand. I was appalled when two thirds of the women in the group stood up. I decided that the men in Reubens never went in search of a wife but waited for an eligible lady teacher to come to town.

I shouldn't laugh because I followed suit and found the love of my life, Vincent Scott, in that special little town. It took him two years to decide he didn't want to be a swinging bachelor but a happily married man. When he returned from the service the fall of '46 he bragged he didn't plan to ever marry. All that changed February of 1948 and we had 64 wonderful years before he passed away.

Vincent Scott

Back to memories of Reubens school: One of my favorites is the time I sent homework with a bookkeeping student and when I told her it was still incorrect her mother came to school and told me "I know it is right because I did it myself".

Another goody was the boy, Lester, with all thumbs in typing. He asked to take his work home because his older sister had a typewriter he could use to catch up his work. He came back to school with perfect lessons and claimed he had typed them himself. His mother backed him up. (His sister Betty was an excellent typist).

One year when we were decorating for a Sadie Hawkins dance one of the boys offered his dad's pickup to go pick up hay bales from a neighbor's field. We had hardly gotten started around the extremely rough field when three fenders fell off. I was horrified thinking what it would cost me to repair the pickup but Kenneth assured me not to worry because the fenders were just hay wired on and his dad, Floyd, would fix them again. Apparently, it had happened before.

Dorothy and Vincent Scott Wedding
Attendants: The Skeltons with Loretta and Billie

Another unforgettable memory took place in Consumer Economics class while making a fabric scrapbook. Each student was to bring fabric for the project; however, the boys were not very interested and had not contributed to the cause. One day Don Curry and Chuck Wood came to class and said they had a surprise for me as they had a fur sample for the book – a tail off a live cat!

Pat Howerton was color blind (I did not know it at the time) and the other students would point at his socks and laugh. He told me his problem and from then on when the kids teased him, he would look at me and I would shake my head yes or no letting him know if his socks matched.

The school had an old, old copy machine that operated with black ink. It managed to throw ink all over the person operating it so my grandmother made me some smock aprons to wear to protect my dresses. I had students, Kenneth Simmons, Pat Howerton and Robert Skelton that were good mechanics and kept this old machine running so we could publish the school paper on a regular basis; actually they were better repairmen than typists.

Our superintendent, Leo Rieman, had arthritis and I know he must have suffered each and every day but he always had a smile and was a special person and very good administrator. I felt very lucky to have worked with him because he supported his staff and always had time for them. He and his wife, Rosa Mae, were special people and were appreciated in our community.

I coached girl's basketball and although I had played ball I wasn't the best of coaches. We may not have won many games but we had lots of spirit and lots of fun. They were a great bunch of good sports. Maybe we didn't get enough practice time. With 45-minute periods, it took 15 minutes to walk to the gym down town, 15 minutes to practice and 15 minutes to walk back to school and the next class.

I directed several plays that both the students and I enjoyed but one of the most fun things we did was a musical "A Pretty Girl is Like a Melody". We made costumes including large picture hats out of tag board with all the trimmings.

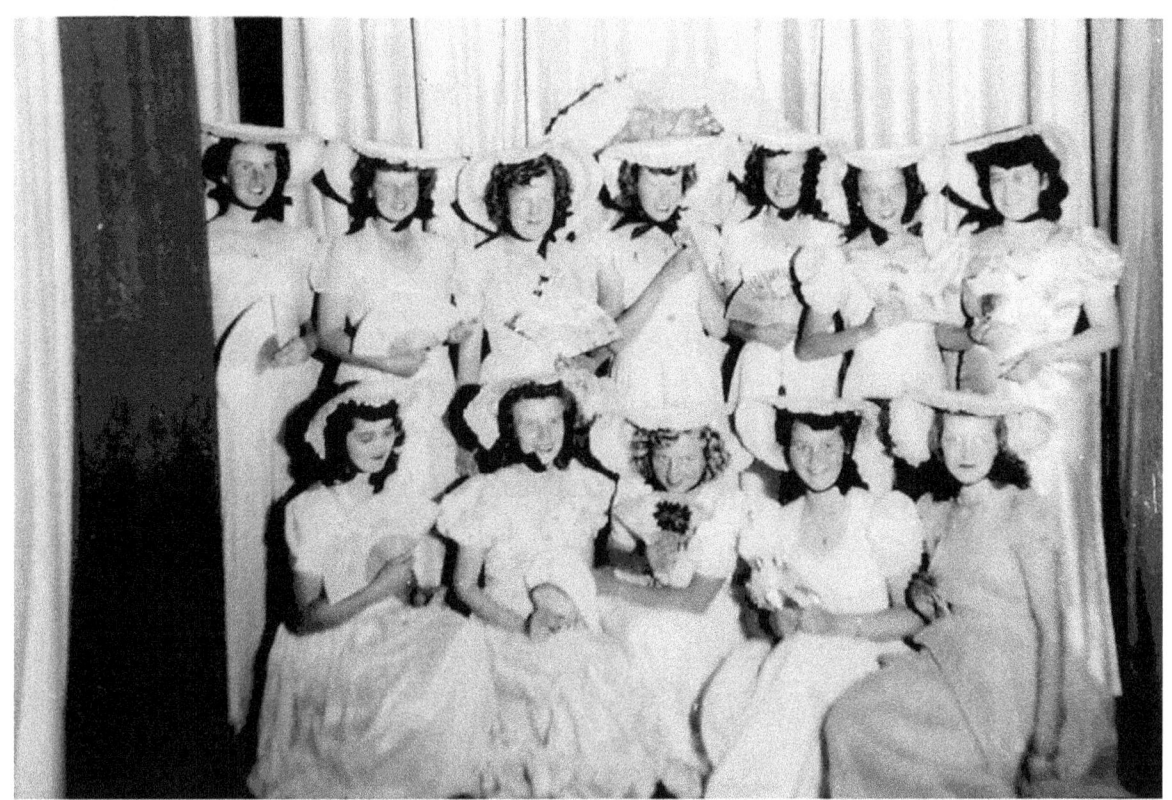

A Pretty Girl is Like a Melody

We always made a big event of the formal dances and proms. One year we worked late one night scotch taping crepe paper streamers together to reach across the width of the gym to look like a pretty sky. The next morning we were to go down and add the fresh blossoms and final touches for the big night. The dampness of the night air in the gym  had let all the scotch tape loosen and the streamers were hanging over the wire we used to hold the sky up. Back to square one and getting it all ready for dance time, but we made it.

I could go on and on but I am sure this book does not have time for that many memories. As you can see, I loved Reubens School and all the teachers, students and parents that went with it. My time at the school didn't end with my two years under contract but after I was married and had my family, I still had the pleasure of substituting. There were several of us former teachers that had the fun of going back and helping when needed. It was great watching the students I had taught, grow up, move on in life, marry, have families and come back to visit. I admit it made me feel old seeing them all mature so fast but it was still great to get to be a part of their lives.

I am 86 years old and still bless the day I accepted the teaching position at Reubens School at 19 years of age and married a wonderful man and his family. MEMORIES ARE FOREVER is a very true statement.

Note: I did receive more education through correspondence and extension classes.

During my tenure, Birdie West who was very artistic re-designed the current school mascot, "The Demon," turning him into a cute, loveable little mascot.

The 1950 Demon's Pitchfork

CLASS OF 1948

Bill Wood

Spouse: Adabelle Dickinson Wood

Do you remember the time Kenneth Simmons decided if he took the screws out of the circular grate (up stairs–high school level) and set it off to the side, that Mr. Shawn (the Superintendent) would step on it and fall all the way down to the basement? Well, guess who did it. The next Monday morning, Kenneth, bless his soul, came to school with a big black eye, lots of scratches and a big "D" imprinted in his forehead. He had fallen down the ventilator shaft and went through the boards at the bottom and landed on Mr. Marquam's bed in front of the furnace. Can you imagine what we called him with that big "D" on his forehead?

And do you remember that Laurine Skelton was the only kid in school that could kick the football over the school house?

CLASS OF 1950

Birdie West

(Written by her Sister, Frances West Holdorf)

Birdie West

Recording Tucano language in Columbia. Betty Welch center, Birdie West

Birdie attended school at Reubens September 1945 until graduation in 1950. Our family moved to Reubens, the summer of 1945, from Vancouver, WA and purchased the Reubens Garage and home from Ladru Misner. We enjoyed living in this quaint town which included a grocery store, pool hall, post office, clothing store, hardware store, city hall, garage/service station, Grange Hall, church, railroad station and two grain elevators. Birdie was in the 8th grade when we first went to school in Reubens. We enjoyed our short walk to school, especially on the old board sidewalks.

Attending school at Reubens was a very positive experience for Birdie. Since reading was one of her favorite pastimes, she loved school, and graduated as Valedictorian of her class. She was well known for her artistic ability, working on the yearbook, school paper and decorating for various school activities. She enjoyed drama and girls chorus. Birdie was very grateful for her teachers and all the life-long friends she made there.

Betty Welch & Birdie West In Columbia

She went on to Whitworth College (University now) in Spokane, majoring in Education. She graduated with honors being selected for "Who's Who in American Colleges and Universities". After teaching school for six years, she obeyed the Lord's call into full-time service, joining Wycliffe Bible Translators. She and her co-worker Betty Welch worked with the Tucanos in Colombia, South America for over 40 years, learning their unwritten language, getting it in written form and eventually translating the New Testament into their language. Birdie and Betty saw the completion of the New Testament for the Tucanos in Brazil.

In October 2008, Birdie went to Tyler, TX to help her co-worker Betty after lung surgery. In November, Birdie became very ill, having difficulty breathing. She steadily grew worse and had emergency surgery the day after Thanksgiving to remove a cancerous thyroid. She recovered nicely from surgery, but by late December, the cancer had spread to her trachea. She lived two weeks, going to her heavenly home on January 12, 2009. Many Wycliffe friends visited her during her final days. She maintained a happy, positive outlook on life to the very end. Her greatest desire was for all of her dear friends and acquaintances to come to know her Lord, Jesus Christ. (December 18, 1931–January 12, 2009).

Frank West Family
- Birdie - Jessie - Frank - Francie

Everta Jeanne Leeper Thomason

Spouse: Bill Thomason

I have good memories of attending Reubens school for 12 years and graduated in 1950. Those years were the best of the best. We were taught to respect our teachers. If we messed up we knew we would be disciplined, and then we would catch it again when we got home. Schools are so much different now. I remember the paddle hanging in Mr. Rieman's office and that put the fear in me.

When I was in high school the most daring thing we did was to skip school on Veterans Day. We thought it should be a holiday. So we climbed out of the upstairs windows. Now I wonder, how did we do that?. From the second floor it was quite a distance to the ground.

I have a picture of Birdie climbing out the window. I was surprised that she would skip school. First thing in the morning Mr. Rieman would come in for the pledge of allegiance and a Bible reading. So he had a surprise when the student body room was empty. I can see his eyes twinkle in spite of what we had done.

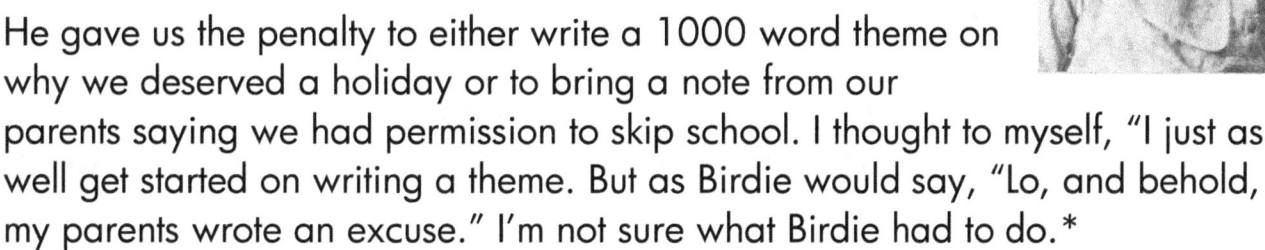

He gave us the penalty to either write a 1000 word theme on why we deserved a holiday or to bring a note from our parents saying we had permission to skip school. I thought to myself, "I just as well get started on writing a theme. But as Birdie would say, "Lo, and behold, my parents wrote an excuse." I'm not sure what Birdie had to do.*

I am grateful for all my old friends and the many new friends I now have in Lewiston. It truly was a good move for me. God has blessed me richly. Of course, Bill was my best friend and I miss him every single day.

Comment: This (memory book) is a neat idea. It will be fun to read the different letters.

*Footnote: "I'm not sure what Birdie had to do."

> (Information from Birdie's sister, Frances West Holdorf: *I remember well the night our parents had a Very Serious Talk with Birdie, after she skipped school. Birdie told me later that the only reason she skipped school was because she didn't want to be the only one left there. Knowing our parents, I believe they must have written a note, expressing their disapproval of Birdie's actions yet explaining the reason why she skipped school. I don't think she ever skipped school again.*)

I started school at the age of five and graduated when seventeen in 1950. In the first grade I was scared of my own shadow. Things continued to get better as I continued.

Mr. Rieman

There are two things that stand out in my mind while in grade school. In the middle class room, fourth, fifth and sixth we had to memorize several different poems and recite them before the class There were two that were my favorites, "Trees" and "The Village Black Smith". It took a little push to get me up front but I did memorize them and enjoyed it.

Mr. Code (not sure about his name) built a wood boat large enough for the Geography class and we would go and sit in the boat for class. I thought it was great fun.

Mr. Rieman was superintendent of every thing. All the high school kids would tell us about the large paddle that Mr. Rieman had hanging on his wall in the office. The thing I remember about Mr. Rieman was that he could be very stern but would often have a twinkle in his eyes while doing it. I can still see that twinkle today. Mr. Rieman was a true gentleman.

Made it into high school and through initiation. Have you ever worn a scratchy gunny sack all day? Not fun! In high school there was always something fun going on. Class Plays, dances and the big one, the Junior Prom. Our theme was Star Dust. I can remember cutting out stars.

That was my first date with Bill. Little did we know we would spend the next 56 years together. We had a wonderful life and did a lot of fun things, such as camping, walking and trailering. We took several trailer trips with the Huntleys seeing some beautiful country in Utah. Mostly we just enjoyed each other.

We didn't always stick to studies. One Halloween night we went out to see if we could find some trouble to get into. We came upon a brown horse in a pasture and tied him up and painted white polka dots on the horse. Next morning Mr. Rieman called us all into the office and asked if we had tipped some bee hives over. We gave a big sigh of relief and were free to go.

Everta
Baccalaureate 1950

We respected our teachers as we should have. There were rules to follow and if we didn't we were in trouble at school and bigger trouble when we got home.

Please pray for our schools. Pray that we can get the Bible back in the class room and have a daily reading and prayer time

My Life after attending 12 years at Reubens Public School

In the fall of 1950 Bill and I were married in the Presbyterian Church, now a Community Church in Reubens. Records show we were the first wedding to be held in the Church. At the time of our wedding the Church was being renovated. We moved some paint cans and swept up some sawdust and went ahead with the wedding.

Bergdorf 1953

We also celebrated our 50th Anniversary at the Church with family and friends. We had the same bridal party and soloist there as we had in 1950. In 2006 the Church celebrated One Hundred years, something Bill helped plan and really enjoyed. Bill was killed in an automobile accident in the fall of 2006

We raised two sons in Reubens, Dennis and Kelly. Dennis lives in Bandon, OR, and Kelly lives in Craigmont ID. Both started school in Reubens and later went to Highland in Craigmont due to school consolidation. They graduated from Highland. Both participated in sports at Highland Dad and Mom never missed a game! That was the best time of our lives.

Everta & Bill, Kelly & Dennis

My grandchildren all live in Bend, OR, with the exception of Kelly's 2 sons. Scott is an art director in Portland, OR. He's very skilled in the arts. Isaiah is in the US Air Force. He is a navigator and flies from the base in Kansas to the airbase in Gatar (also spelled Qatar) a small independent country on the Arabian Peninsula. Something he wanted to do since he was 3 years old was to fly. He is getting to see a lot of the country.

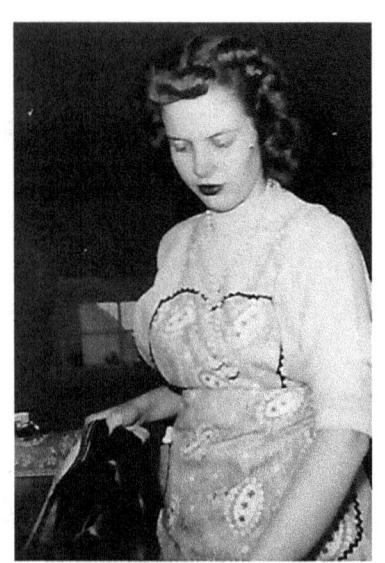

Happy Homemaker

I'm a proud grand mother of 8 grandchildren and 7 great grandchildren. Thank goodness for computers! The girls keep me updated with information and lots of pictures. The youngest is 7 months old and I would so like to get my hands on him. Smile!

As for me I have lived in Lewiston for 7 years and Love it. I have a new house, garden, flowers etc. and have everything I need except for my husband.

Bill has a long history in Reubens. His first love was the Reubens Presbyterian Church where he served as treasurer for 27 years. He served on the Elder Board and held every office in the Church at one time or another. I overheard one person say, "Bill is the Church" That about sums it up. (To which this editor says, "Amen, Sister!)

In 1964, Bill started the Sausage Feed when the Church needed a new roof and planned on just having it until the roof was paid off. This March was the 50th year for the feed and it's still going strong. Our son, Kelly has taken over the leadership to honor his Dad.

Full Up with Sausage, Pancakes and Eggs
Well Worth theTrip up the Hill

In 1953 Bill was elected chairman of the board of the village of Reubens. He served in that capacity until the 60s when the State changed all villages to the Council–Mayor form of government. Bill was elected Mayor in the first election and held that position for 42 years. He was always a dad first, taking the boys hunting and fishing, etc. His cemetery stone says, "The Perfect DAD."

Mildred Timme

I transferred from Gifford High School to Reubens, where I attended for one year, my senior year. At Reubens my teachers were Leo Rieman, Superintendent, Mort Curtis and Leona Wilson. Our class motto was "To the Stars Through Difficulties". Our class colors were Blue and Silver and our class flowers were pink and white roses.

Special memories I have of my time at Reubens were playing basketball and the Senior Sneak to Seattle, Washington and Vancouver, B.C.

Leona Becker Armstrong

Spouse: Tom Armstrong

1946 my family moved to Reubens and it was my entry into High School with a full student body the same size as a class I'd previously been in. I had a wonderful four years at school. Our class was small in number but mighty in friendship and loyalty to each other. We started out with five girls and one boy. Our senior year we gained two girls from Gifford, giving us seven girls and one boy.

Mr. Rieman was such a good guiding force for all-of us, he had much foresight and guidance and help in whatever endeavor that any of the students cared to take in their lives.

These were the days when girls always wore dresses to school-not the jeans and shorts you see nowadays. I always liked sports, so one time the boys wanted to have a football team, they were short of boys in high school, so I and a couple of other girls approached Mr. Rieman to see if we could have permission to wear jeans and be part of the team. Mr. Rieman replied that this was no game for young ladies and he would not approve of this.

I enjoyed Ping-Pong so much and Bill and Chuck Woods were so good at it that it was fun to get to school early and have some games before school started. Our school did quite well in girl's basketball even if we did not get much time to practice as we had to walk to town and back each PE period. I was very lucky and was able to set the high point record for the school with 42 points. I broke the record set by Laura Scott years before.

The thing that impressed me most was how we were able to have so much fun with special parties -by pushing all the desks aside in the study room and play games such as drop the hankie, flying Dutchman, even the alumni boys at home would come to the party and we had such a good time. We finished up the evening with deserts and juice and NO ALOCHOL and had a wonderful time.

Small schools knew how to have fun. Many of our graduates went on to some very rewarding jobs and seeing the world.

Calista Arlene Brackett Moore

Spouse: Martin Moore

My first school was in Lookout, Idaho and my second in Reubens. I liked Reubens; the teachers and the kids were all nice. It was fun playing basketball, and my granddad Bill Marquam was the school janitor for years. He also was the wood shop teacher and taught us how to work with wood. I was named after my grandmother Calista Marquam.

I also liked having my 4-H calf. I got to go to Spokane, Washington to show the calf. I am grateful for having been a student at Reubens.

Gerrie (Meier) Johnson

Spouses: Carl E. Johnson (deceased-July 1985)

Floyd W. Harvey (deceased-August 2010)

I started school at Reubens when I was in the 6th grade, so probably would have been 11 or 12 years old. I attended Reubens until I graduated from high school in 1950.

Special school memories during my time at Reubens:

I remember Birdie West and I working in Principal Rieman's office on the mimeograph machine in our Senior year, and we decided to paint his telephone receiver with mimeograph ink. I think Mr. Rieman was very surprised when he asked whoever painted his phone to go clean it up and Birdie and I got up to do so as we were two of the top students in that class.

I also remember at our graduation when Claude Webb, Frank West, Charles Brackett and my Dad, Arthur Meier sang (I don't remember what song), but it made me cry.

I am grateful for being in a small school where we were able to know everyone.

Gerrie Johnson's life after graduating from RHS in 1950.

Gerrie, Leona, Everta, Mildred

I attended Kinman's Business University and graduated from there in 1951.

Worked at Nez Perce Tractor for a short time before marrying Carl (Johnny) Johnson in 1952. We had four children, Debbie, Guy, Brad & Lori, who all reside in Lewiston, except Lori, who lives in Eugene, Oregon.

Each of my children had two kids-a boy and girl, except Brad, who has two boys. So I have eight grandchildren and seven great grandchildren. I worked as a legal secretary for thirty-five years. Johnny taught at Lapwai High School, eventually becoming principal. He died from colon cancer in 1985.

In 1994 I married Floyd Harvey. We traveled to several other countries during our marriage. Floyd passed away in 2010. I still live in Lewiston and retired at the end of 1994. I attend the Orchards United Methodist Church and am quite active in it. After Floyd died I went back to using the last name of Johnson as I had never changed any of my financial records and my children were Johnsons.

CLASS OF 1951

Nancy Teats Flint

Spouse: Donald Keith Flint

Nancy Ellen Wuicich-Teats Flint was born in Cheyenne, Wyoming to Pauline Warren Gilson (BD 9-30-1913 at Lewiston, Ida.) and George N. Wuicich (BD 8-25-1903 in Yugoslavia). Her Parents divorced after a turbulent marriage.

July 1939 Pauline went to work for Philip Augustus Teats and Pauline and Phil married in 1940. Nancy's wonderful parents had 5 more children (Susan Kathleen; Michael Philip; Murray Lewis; Ted Allen; Daniel Leon).

I attended grade school and high school at Reubens. I loved learning, had some good friends and endured teasing. I had good teachers who taught me well. In high school, Glee Club was a highlight. The other things I enjoyed were learning to square dance, picnics, parties and band. I have many other good memories that are too numerous to mention.

Growing up on the farm was a wonderful wholesome life. After high school I attended the University of Idaho for 3 years with a geological engineering major. In 1953, at the U of I, I met Donald Keith Flint and we married in August,-1954. After a brief honeymoon Don went to Boston to serve 2 years in alternative service while I returned to the farm.

In May, 1955, Lissa Ruth was born in Lewiston; she lived 4 days. In January 1956 I went to Washington D. C where I commuted to Beltsville, MD. to work in the map division of U.S. Ag. Research Center. In August 1956 Don joined me in Greenbelt, MD, and in April, 1957, Keith Philip was born. In September of 1957 we moved to Idaho so Don could finish his BA degree at the U. of I.

In September of 1958 we moved to Philadelphia where Don attended 4 years of seminary. While there 2 sons were born, Jonathan Paul and Clell Andrew After a short pastorate we moved in May, 1964 to Hamtramck, MI. where Don served a few years as a home missionary. We moved to Detroit and Don went back to school to get his MSW. After this Don served both in social work and the church. Don retired from the church in 1995 (we moved to Sterling Heights, MI.) and from social work in 1997. Don continues to supply preach every Sunday.

While living in Detroit I worked from 1975-78 at Market Opinion Research (in the map division). From 1979-85 I was a volunteer teacher of oil painting and water colors. I continue painting, sewing, and some writing. Blessings to all!

Grace Moore Weinert

Spouse: Paul Weinert

I attended school at Reubens only my last two years of high school. Our family moved quite often.

Special School Memories:

I enjoyed the close relationship of the whole high school student body. I will always remember our Geometry class, putting ourselves through it. We had study hall together and each of us worked what he or she could and then explained to the rest. That way we would get most of the problems done.

Paul and Grace Moore Weinert

I remember how much fun we had putting on plays and skits. Sometimes we would write the skits ourselves which was very enjoyable.

I am grateful for the teachers who helped broaden my life and all the companionship from many of my friends. I will always be grateful to George Hayes who coached our girl's basketball team and made us eat left-handed. (That helped me in many ways, including being able to paint our house with both hands.)

CLASS OF 1952

Raydene Cannon Willows

Memories of Reubens

Our family came to Reubens when my grandparents Ross and Emma Russell bought a farm on the edge of town. One year after Christmas their farm house burned to the ground, so they purchased a house in town. My mother, Alice Russell Cannon and her sisters graduated from Reubens High School. The sisters were Irma, Mary and Margaret. Margaret married Bob Lay, a teacher at Reubens High School.

My dad's family moved to Reubens when he was in the 8th grade. His parents were John and Nora Cannon. Grandpa worked at Fisher's market in Reubens. Grandma was a great cook and prepared meals for the train crews when they came to Reubens. Those men really looked forward to those wonderful meals.

Grandpa Ross Russell (mother's dad) died in Aug. of 1933. Grandma Emma Russell moved to Lewiston in 1936 and my parents bought her home in Reubens. It had indoor plumbing, one of the few in the town that had indoor plumbing at that time. That was a very nice family home.

Glen and Raydene Cannon

Dad had a brother, Everett. We all called him Uncle Big and he married Kate Curry. They had a small ranch near Gifford. Big and Kate had three children, Lois and Glen. That family moved down to Clarkston and there they had the third child, a girl named Carma Jean.

Dad had a sister, Aunt Ethel. She married Louie Lunders and they added a set of twins to the family tree, Leonard and Louis, who also attended RHS for three years.

My mother and her sister Mary played basketball all 4 years of High school and they won most of their games. My brothers R. Russell (Russ) Cannon born in 1925 and Lynn E Cannon born in 1927 were very busy with school activities. When there was a home game the boys who lived on farms would stay at our house so they would be on time for the game. Our house was always a welcome place to our friends and family.

My parents owned the creamery and service station. Dad hauled merchandise for the grocery store and the Reubens Supply. Before I started school, Dad closed in the back of his truck to use it as a school bus. I had fun riding with him to pick up the kids. Mom ran the creamery and service station.

I remember when they started the hot lunch program at school. Lora Scott Skelton was the cook and the food was delicious. Our teachers were Miss Taylor and Barbara Mjelde. They were both very special to those of us in the 1st, 2nd and 3rd grades. We had many delicious Sunday dinners cooked by Daisy Scott and Mom at the Scott farm. That was like a second home to us. I remember riding the train to visit my grandmother in Lewiston.

We left Reubens in October 1942 and lived in Boise for 2 months while dad went to welding school and then on to Casper, Wyoming. In Casper Dad worked at the air base doing maintenance on the aircraft.

Russ graduated from High School at Casper and his class of guy's all enlisted in the Army the next day. Lynn was in ROTC and looked great in his uniform. We moved back to Idaho in Aug of 1943 and I graduated from Lewiston High School in 1952.

Reubens was great place to begin our family life.

Joanne (Joan) Lewis

I attended school at Reubens 1st through 3rd grades.

Special memories while I lived at Reubens:

My Dad, Vernon Lewis, was the railroad depot agent. We moved from Reubens, June 1943, to Fenn. My Dad passed away September 1943.

My best friends were Laurine Skelton Nightingale and Delores Howerton Harrington. Laurine's Dad had the grain elevator across the railroad tracks and we had lot of good times playing together.

Annie Webb lived down the hill from the depot and was a senior citizen. I would go to the store for her and I have some wonderful memories of the time I spent visiting with her. She gave me some of her doll dishes and I still have them. She always had pansies growing by her front porch. She told me pansies mean friendship. I put pansies on the graves of my friends that have passed away in memory of Anna.

When it snowed Mr. Dieckhoff would pick up the kids that lived in town in his sled pulled by his horse. We had to sing to him on the way to school.

Laurine and Joan

When I was in the 4th grade we moved to Clarkston, Washington. I was scared the first day because there were so many kids. When I walked into the room, the first person I saw was Lois Cannon whom I knew from Reubens. What a blessing to see her!

I am very grateful for the people who have kept the Reubens Reunion going. It's so nice to keep in touch with classmates and friends.

I graduated from Clarkston High School in 1952.

Laurine Skelton Nightingale

Spouse Jesse Nightingale (deceased)

Sixty years since graduation really taxes the memory but with the help of annuals, (year books) flashbacks are coming through. To those of you who attended R. H. S. during this era this writing will not reveal new information but hopefully perk fond memories. Perhaps it will be of more interest to those reading it in the future. Details may not be exact, but as I best remember them.

Reubens was a thriving little farming community on the west edge of the Camas Prairie during my growing up years. My Dad, James Skelton, was mayor of the town for over 30 years and the manager of a grain elevator for as many years. My Mom, Malvine, was a teacher by profession until her marriage. A brother, James, was twelve years older than I.

When I left Reubens in 2001, having spent my lifetime there, I was considered one of the "old timers". At that time the population had dwindled to about 80 people. The school had been consolidated into the Craigmont system. Many other "old timers" had retired as family farms had also been consolidated. The business section of town had disappeared and employment was at a minimum.

My formal education of 12 years was within the walls of that small, prairie school. There was no pre-school or kindergarten back then and perhaps one half day was spent visiting the classroom before the beginning of the school year. I cannot claim K-12.

Laurine's 14th Birthday Party

My life long friend Rena Brackett and I began our education together continuing through graduation. Our first grade teacher was Miss Mejelde whom I thought was beautiful. During that school term of 1941-42, the entire school had a modest enrollment of 57 students. The first three Primary grades, were together in one room with one teacher for 14 students. The 4th, 5th and 6th consisted of 9 students. The 7th and 8th grade had 11 students.

In the high school there were eight seniors, three juniors, six sophomores and six freshmen. The faculty consisted of the Superintendent and two teachers. The teachers filled void spaces perhaps as band teacher or coach wherever and whenever needed, whether qualified or not. I mention this as times have changed so much but education received in those days emphasized sound basics that were and still are extremely important fundamentals to a good education. Technology is great but the foundation, the three "R's" of education, is crucial.

1952 High Achievers

World War II was just beginning and the entire country was in disarray. "War Bonds" were a big thing and every student was encouraged to buy saving stamps to fill a book that would be turned into a government bond very similar to today's savings bonds.

Wilma Taylor was my second grade teacher and in third grade I had three teachers beginning with Wilma Taylor then Marie Webb and finally Shirley Laird. Marie and Shirley were substitute teachers married to local farm boys. We were fortunate to have had local educators available. World War II was in full swing and there was a shortage of teachers. I am sure Reubens was so small it did not hold much attraction at that time.

As for grade school, school was school, nothing extremely outstanding. I competed in several spelling bees, received a certificate for never being late or absent and bugged the boys to let me play football with them. I was a real tomboy at heart. I took home an average report card, was told to respect the teachers and if I got in trouble at school I would also be punished at home. In sixth grade I was the tallest girl in grade school and was nicknamed String Bean. That growth spurt didn't last long for others soon caught up or passed me.

Time has taken its toll on the town and the field of education is nothing as it once was. This is what I remember from those bygone days. There were no cement walks back then, only wooden sidewalks throughout town and leading to the school. There are remainders of them in that area still today. In the spring, a creek that ran under the sidewalk would overflow and provide much entertainment, often causing students to be tardy for school and late arriving home after school. In the fall we would pick apples along this same route. The trees still bear fruit. Life then was simple and good.

I envied the country kids who could ride the school bus everyday. The first bus I remember was nothing more than a station wagon with seats the length of the back compartment rather than across the vehicle. It couldn't have held many passengers. Living in town I was denied the privilege of riding m one.

Hot lunch program was unheard of. Everyone brought their own lunch, usually in a tin lunch box that also held a thermos bottle of milk. Most sandwiches were made of home made bread. The first school lunch program consisted of hot soup. It was prepared upstairs on a hot plate, in a room no larger than a closet. This was to enhance the lunch box sandwich.

At that time there were no Government programs providing food or commodities. Later, the ladies of the Reubens Community Club would preserve food to be used for the lunch program. Produce came from individual gardens and was canned in glass jars using a hot water bath method or pressure cooker. I remember my mother pressure cooking chickens and also green beans. Once when she was removing the half gallon jars of beans from the pressure cooker one of the jars exploded, sending the lid skyward and into the

Cellotex ceiling board where the indent remained forever. Another year the ladies prepared the food for canning and took it to Lapwai to a commercial canning plant there. The food came back in tin cans looking very professional.

High School was a blast, except for having to study. Throughout high school the class of "52" were the "doers." Of course, it took the whole student body plus the community to produce a successful event. Parents and Grandparents participated in the school dances, especially the Prom. They supported all events and it was more like one large family than a school.

Senior Dinner At Lenora's, 1952

Our junior prom theme was Old Fashioned Garden. We spent evening after evening making flowers from crepe paper at the home of our class advisor, George Hayes, to decorate for this very special event. He and his wife Dorothy were great teachers. She taught music, drama and English. He taught English, P.E., Art, and Journalism. Other teachers during my high school were Lenora O'Brien, Duane Cole, Mort Curtis, Alice Carter and Leona Wilson. Leo Rieman was Superintendent during our high school years and a more dedicated man was not to be found. He was an inspiration to each and every student and to the community.

Basketball was the competitive sport. The girls had a team and the rules were very different from today's. It was definitely a no contact sport back then. Because of the small enrollment, Sam Curry volunteered to be the boxing coach, when there were not enough boys to form a basketball team.

Archery, tennis, volley ball and softball were offered during P.E. whenever a teacher was willing to oversee it. The Gym was not attached to the school but was located several blocks away. We seldom had transportation so often ran the distance never thinking twice about it.

The gym was a wooden structure with a stage area at one end and two dressing rooms behind that. The opposite end of the building had stairs on one side leading to the balcony with one long row of benches for seating. The opposite side had a wooden ladder attached to the wall as the means of reaching the balcony. The men and boys mostly occupied that side.

A large crude looking wood burning stove provided heating at that end of the gym floor opposite the stage. A metal pipe structure protected the public from getting too close to the hot stove. It would not pass OSHA inspection today.

Senior Sneak 1952

In the dressing rooms there were showers and restrooms, which were no more than an attached outhouse. These rooms were heated with small wood burning stoves also. Very unsophisticated compared to today's state of art activity centers.

Every community activity was held in the gym building. Everything from a boxing bout to a prom, a box social or the Ladies Community Club bazaar was held in this building. There was a kitchen area attached to one side of the building, so this was the place to be for social activities in the community.

The gym was probably my favorite hangout for I spent many hours there. I loved basketball, whether competing or as a spectator. Other fine memories of cheerleading, choir and band concerts were created in this building along with school plays, dances and especially the proms. The Prom was the social event of the year.

The senior sneak was the grand finale for twelve years of school. What fun we had at a resort in Oregon during spring break in 1952. We were definitely small town kids enjoying new surroundings with our chaperones Mrs. O'Brien and Lora Skelton, who provided transportation.

A year after graduation I married a farmer from the Craigmont area, Jesse Nightingale. We lived near Craigmont for two years then moved to Reubens where we remained until 2001. Farming was our livelihood and Reubens was a wonderful place to raise our four children. Steven, Cathy, David and Sherri who enjoyed the serenity of rural America as I had. I prepared hot lunches for a few years at Reubens, then at Craigmont after school consolidation.

2006 Reunion
Birdie   Laurine   Clarice   Francie

Politics held a fascination for me. In 1980 I ran and was elected to the office of County Commissioner from District 3 representing Reubens, Craigmont and Winchester, an office I held for the next 20 years. Upon retiring we relocated to the Cottonwood area where Jesse passed away in 2003. I continue to live on a farm near the outskirts of town.

Good health has allowed me to keep busy being involved with the grandchildren's activities, camping and fishing with family and friends, volunteering at the public library and with other community events. Life is Good. I am so blessed.

I am grateful for a wonderful life in Reubens with great memories of school and the community, but most of all, life long friendships with wonderful people that I cherish. It was a great place to grow up and also to raise my family. The freedoms I enjoyed are priceless. May it never end.

To Frances, my class mate, for having the inspiration for this Memory book then seeing it through publication. You always had great ideas with a desire and drive to see them completed. Thank you so much. God Bless.

Howard Stolte

Spouse: Jeanette Springston Stolte

I came to Reubens my sophomore year due to school consolidations. I started school at Fairview, a one room school outside of Gifford. For some reason I couldn't remember my first grade teachers name, and my classmates said it was Miss Robinson. There were ten students in eight grades. I went there for seven years, the eighth and freshman years at Gifford. The students east of town went to Reubens and the rest went to Culdesac.

Special school memories during my time in Reubens:

The fun times we had writing our plays with the help of Mrs. Hayes. The time we put Francie's Model A on a snow drift, and her comment was "YOU GUYS !!". Remembering the activities in the old gym, the fun we had doing our Junior Prom.

J am grateful for Mr. Reiman and all the teachers who helped me with school. Also for the community who accepted us. The class of 1952 will always be special in my mind-THANK YOU!

Frances L. West Holdorf

Spouse: Charles Keith Holdorf

Frances Lorraine West

Our family moved from Vancouver, WA to Reubens during the summer of 1945. My father and mother, Frank and Jessie West purchased the Reubens Garage and home from Ladru Misner. During the process of moving, we lived temporarily in the parsonage next to the church. (That small building was later added on to the remodeled church for storage and a Sunday school room.) We liked the uniqueness of this small town with its board sidewalks.

We enjoyed the sight and sounds of the steam locomotive, chugging through Reubens. Riding the train across Camas Prairie over the trestles to Grangeville or through the tunnels down the canyon to go to Lewiston was a great adventure. Our family felt very welcome in this town and farming community. It was great fun visiting our friends living on the farms.

Birdie, my sister, was in the 8th grade and I was in the 6th grade when we started school in Reubens. We liked walking to school and going home for lunch. Just inside the front door of the school was the broad staircase leading up to the high school. I remember how we (grade school kids) would try to sneak up the stairs before a high school student would yell, "Down stairs!"

At the foot of the stairs was the bell rope Mr. Marquam would let us pull to ring the school bell. Great fun! Our 7th and 8th grade teacher, Bernice Bennett, was very

Frank West Family
- Birdie - Jessie - Frank - Francie

patient with us. She prepared us well for the 8th grade exams required for entrance into high school.

High school was fun, with all the activities such as playing basketball, cheerleading, being in drama productions, working on the school paper and annuals, singing in the girls' chorus and playing trombone in the band. I always enjoyed riding the school bus to games and other activities. In my senior year, I was honored as Queen of the Lewis County Fair in Nez Perce. (Reubens turn to select the queen; princesses were from the other schools in the county.)

It was, also, an honor to be Valedictorian of our graduating class.

Our teachers were outstanding for a small school. Mr. and Mrs. George Hayes contributed much to our education. Mr. Hayes was a great basketball coach and Mrs. Hayes was an excellent musician, directing our band and girls chorus. I developed a love for classic literature in her English classes.

Mr. Rieman was an outstanding superintendent/ principal/ teacher, as well as a good friend to all. Once when he and his wife, Rosa May visited our family, he made a recording of Birdie and me singing. Watching him make this 78RPM phonograph record was a fascinating experience.

Each morning, in study hall, Mr. Rieman read to us from the Bible. A blessing we weren't aware of then! In a few short years that privilege would be taken from our schools. Then remember our punishment for misbehaving? Writing themes!

One morning we came to school and saw footprints up the wall, across the ceiling and down the opposite wall of the study hall. Of course the boys who did this had to write a theme on why we do not walk on the walls or ceiling. I wish we could have read some of those wonderful, creative themes! Mr. Rieman had a great sense of humor, so I'm sure he had many a laugh reading them.

During my junior and senior years, I had a little Model A Ford coupe to drive. One time I was working after school on the yearbook. Some of the boys thought they would play a trick on me by pushing my car up on a high snow bank made by the snow plow. They were waiting to see what I would do when I saw it.

Were they in for a surprise! My little Ford, with chains on it, managed well down the bank and onto the road without any trouble. I have many fond memories of my years spent at Reubens: horse back riding at the Brackett's ranch, sleigh rides on horse-drawn sleighs, skating on the ponds and enjoying the freedom of country living!

Our girls' basketball team did very well in our senior year, coached by Duane Cole. My good friend and classmate, Laurine Skelton (now Nightingale) was an excellent forward. We kept passing the ball to her, she couldn't miss the basket! We missed winning the District Championship when we lost to Ferdinand by one point. My experience playing basketball helped me make the varsity team during my freshman year in college.

Before we graduated from high school, our teachers and principal put on a progressive dinner for us seniors. (This time the teachers played a trick on us. At each house, we were served mock meals—not edible, like "Filet of Sole" at Rieman's , an old leather sole topped with catsup). Next, we went to their homes again, enjoying delicious food! Our teachers were lots of fun, as well as good educators who helped prepare us for the future.

I am very grateful for the teachers and the life-long friends made at that small school. Unlike being in a larger school, we had many opportunities to participate in a variety of activities. After graduation, I went to Whitworth College (University) majoring in Elementary Education. I was well prepared for college with the good education I received at Reubens, including the various activities in drama, music and sports.

After receiving my Bachelor of Arts degree in Education at Whitworth and spending the summer as a missionary on the Navajo Indian Reservation in Arizona, I went on to teach in the Parkrose School District in Portland, OR. During my first year of teaching, I met my future husband, Charles "Keith" Holdorf.

He was working as a flight steward on West Coast Airlines, I was traveling on his flight to Portland. Our relationship blossomed with mutual interests in music, drama, nature and our love for God and each other. We enjoyed a few years of flying privileges before Keith went to Portland State to complete his college education, earning his BS degree in Business Administration.

God blessed our union with four wonderful children: Steven; Charlene; twins, Roberta and Rebecca. In 1965 we moved from Portland to Seattle, WA (our present address). Our family enjoyed ministering in music together. We called ourselves the Holdorf Family Singers, ministering in churches, missions, camps and banquets. Being in Seattle, we had the privilege of hosting many foreign students who were studying English. I, also, volunteered teaching ESL (English as a Second Language).

Christmas and New Years (1979-80) my three daughters and I visited my sister, Birdie West (Wycliffe Bible Translator), in Colombia, South America. This was an exciting adventure living with the Tucano people, sleeping in hammocks, riding in a dugout canoe and trying some of their native foods. In 1982, Keith and I enjoyed touring through Germany, Austria, Yugoslavia, Italy, Switzerland and France with Choir of the Sound.

God has blessed us with many happy memories. We still love to return to Reubens, taking care of the home-place, visiting neighbors and attending church there. The Reubens all-school reunions have been a wonderful way to keep in touch with my long-time friends.

My happiest school memories were at Red River and Reubens, Idaho. Starting school at Red River's one-room school gave me an excellent start in my education and was lots of fun. We were a tight-knit community, supporting one another.

We didn't have that same community spirit in the large schools in Vancouver, Washington where we moved to during World War II. So, we found a strong community spirit at Reubens, supporting the school and one another. I am very thankful for the many blessings of this close-knit community and school. The happy memories and life-long friends will be forever treasured in my heart.

Frances (Francie) West Holdorf October 2013

Rosalyn M. Meier Stellmon

Spouse: Bill Stellmon

I attended school at Reubens from the 4th grade through the 11th.

School memories: I always remember Mr. Rieman looking so stern, then turning his back and you could see him chuckling; all the good times I had with my friends, with whom I still feel close to. We all knew each other. I am very grateful for a small school where you got to know everyone. The reunions are great because we get to visit and talk with everyone. Sometimes we only get to see these people once a year (at the reunions). It's nice to keep in touch.

Historical sketch following school days at Reubens:

After my Jr. year in high school, I married Jim McCall just before he was drafted into the Army. A couple of crazy kids in love who thought they had to be together. We spent time in California and Washington D.C. while Jim was in the service. He also, spent 8 months in Germany while I was with my parents.

After the service he worked for Daddy on the farm for a number of years. In that time we had two children, Michelle and Roger. After 16 years we parted ways, Jim going to radio school in California and I got married to Forrest Hall, a professor in civil engineering at the U of I.

We made our home in the country 4 miles east of Viola. We had a very happy life together. All that came to an end when I lost him to colon cancer in 2006. Michelle had a car accident, she went to sleep while driving and ended up in the river near Elk City. That was in 2005, which was only 1 year before Frosty died. It was a very sad time for me losing both of them. However, God has His plans.

Rosalyn and her sweetheart (and husband) Bill Stellmon

Grief is difficult to bear and it takes a long time to recover, but after 5 ½ years God brought someone else into my life. His name is Bill Stillmon and he is also a U of I professor. We have been going to the same Presbyterian Church for over 45 years and knew each other as an acquaintance. This past year and a half we really got to know each other and fell deeply in love. His wife had died 4 years earlier of cancer, too. We were married April 20, 2013. I only have God to thank for my wonderful husband and the happiness we share.

Roger and Peggy (his wife) live in Sandpoint. Roger has his own shop; he is a mechanic and went to school at LC. They have one son, Dale, who is a mortician and works with his grandfather in Sandpoint. Michelle's daughter lives just outside Spokane.

Our families: from left, son Roger McCall, daughter-in-law Peggy, grandson Dale; on the right side, three of Bill's daughters and one son-in-law.

Her name is Rosa and she gave birth to twins, Emmalynne and Skyler, 2 years ago. They are darling. I'm very proud of my family. Roger has been with me through thick and thin. He is one in a million. I must not forget Jack, my Jack Russell Terrier who's been such a joy and helped me through some rough times. He's 5 ½ years old, very sweet and super, super active-so much fun! Again, thank you God for the good life you gave me. I feel very blessed.

CLASS OF 1953

G. Arthur Misner, Jr.

Spouse: Charlotte Ruckman Misner

G. Arthur Misner, Jr. (Art) began first grade in the fall of 1941 at the Melrose one room school until it closed when he was in the fifth grade. The Melrose and Gifford schools consolidated with the Reubens School district about the same time. Art attended the Lewis Clark Normal School teacher training school for the first half of his sixth grade, then transferred to the Reubens School. His 6th, 7th and 8th grade teacher was Mrs. Opal Sisley. His classmates at this time were Clarice Hill, Geneva Huffman and Martha Stolte.

In high school, extracurricular activities were a necessary part of every Reubens HS student's experience. Art played basketball for four years, was a member of the band where he played the clarinet, participated in various parades at the Lewis and Nezperce County Fairs in Lewiston and other locations. He was in the high school plays, yearbook editor, Class officer and Student Body President.

Art has many memories of his good friend, Jimmy Knowlton, and their antics in high school as well as the many visits with Jim, Clarice & family when we were on home leave in the states. Not sure how enamored the children were about it but Jim always wanted to see Art's slides of various places we lived overseas.

1952 Student Body Officers

President
    JIM KNOWLTON
Vice President
    JUNIOR MISNER
Treasurer
    LAURINE SKELTON
Secretary
    CHARLOTTE RUCKMAN

Art enrolled at the University of Idaho in the fall of 1953. He was an International Farm Youth Exchange (IFYE) student to Pakistan in fall of 1956. Art graduated from the University of Idaho, with honors, in 1958 with a degree in agriculture and the American Institute of Foreign Trade in Phoenix (now Thunderbird School of Global Management) in 1960. He received his MBA from Universidad de las Americas in Mexico City in 1970.

Historical Sketch After College:

Art Misner and Charlotte Ruckman were married on August 29, 1959. In 1960, Art joined Rohm and Haas Company in Philadelphia, PA. He was sent on long term assignments overseas. Rohm & Haas sent Art to Japan for a couple months, Charlotte joined him in Manila, Philippines for six months before our Indian visas arrived and we were transferred to Bombay, India for five and a half years.

Our two older daughters were born in Bombay. In 1967, we transferred to Mexico City for three and a half years, youngest daughter born here. We were transferred back to the Philippines in 1970 when Art was named General Manager of Philippine subsidiary for six years. Then, Art became Area Director for 10 Asian countries for seven years.

Art and Charlotte lived overseas for a total of 23 years before returning to San Francisco Bay area in 1984. With their daughters, they enjoyed traveling to numerous countries around the world during their annual home leaves. Art also worked for the city of Oakland for 10 years before retiring in 2000.

Charlotte, in addition to being a mom to three daughters, could be called a professional volunteer. Over the years, she has volunteered with many organizations at home and overseas. She was a founding member of the

American Women's Club of Manila, Philippines and chaired several fundraising activities for St. Luke's Hospital in Manila.

She led a capital campaign and secured scholarship endowments for the women of Alpha Gamma Delta. In 1986, she started as a part- time employee at the nonprofit organization Friends of Oakland Parks and Recreation, and went on to become its executive director. She retired in 2000.

Currently, Art and Charlotte enjoy their summers on the Middle Fork and their winters at a retirement community in Walnut Creek, CA.

Glen Cannon

Spouse: Alice Dellaven Cannon

My name is Glen Cannon and I am married to Alice DeHaven Cannon.

I attended school in Reubens in 1942. My older sister, Lois, started in 1941. We were faithful students until September of 1944, when my family moved us to Clarkston, Washington. I had made it through to the second grade in Reubens. My sister, Lois, passed away in July of 1951.

I graduated in 1953, from Clarkston High School.

Some of the special memories I have while attending school at Reubens are riding in the white and black school bus. Tommy Kelly was our driver. The benches were not padded so the ride could be rough at times. Another memory that I have is of the large swing set that seemed to be real high. I was really afraid to get on it.

The first time I had seen anyone with a cast on his leg was while I was attending school in Reubens. Loren Crow had broken his leg and he was in a cast and on crutches. I was scared that he would fall. Doug Gaut sat in front of me in class and he would bring a "new" toy almost every day to school. The teacher would say before class, "Doug, give me your toys." She had quite a box full by the end of the year.

I am grateful for these memories and the opportunity to meet so many wonderful and neat people while going to school there. The people in that school and who lived in that community were so kind, that I am very proud to say that I was a part of that.

Glen and Alice Cannon

CLASS OF 1954

Don Moore

Spouse: Beulah Sharp Moore

I attended school at Reubens four (4) months, September-December 1949 (Editor's note, 7th Grade). A special memory of my time at Reubens was playing catcher on the softball team. I left during Christmas break because I thought my folks were moving to St. Maries, Idaho. I went on ahead and finished out that year at St. Maries. The next fall I joined them in Clarkston, Washington.

The first half of the 8th grade, I was in Clarkston, the second half, in Lewiston, Idaho. Grades 9-12 I was in Big Horn, Wyoming.

We moved to Lewiston in 1955, I worked at Safeway, then at Potlatch. I married in 1958. We have three (3) children: Marvin, Martin and Diane. We moved to Pasco, Washington, January of 1966 where I worked as an electrician at Boise Cascade Corporation and retired in July 1998.

In December 2011 we sold our home and acreage east of Pasco and are currently living in our 33 foot Newmar Motor Home. We are currently staying on our son's property south of Kennewick. I will be pleasure fishing with my nephew on his boat out of Juneau, Alaska. Besides our three children, we have three grandsons, one granddaughter, one great granddaughter and two great grandsons.

I am grateful for good health, family and travel opportunities to Arizona, Alaska, touring the East Coast and Southern USA. Hopefully I'll be able to attend one of the reunions. Thank you for the invitations.

CLASS OF 1955

Charlotte Ruckman Misner

Spouse: G. Arthur Misner

Charlotte Ruckman began first grade at Reubens in the fall of 1943. My classmates were Fred O'Brien, Donna Mae Leeper, and Jim Brackett. Later Donnie Hill, Richard Becker and Doran Rogers joined our class to make it seven. There were several others who came and went during those twelve years.

I attended Grades 1 thru 12 at the Reubens Public School, located five miles south of my folks place. We rode the bus to and from school every day. Students attended from the town of Reubens (350 Pop.) and the surrounding farming community.

The school elementary and middle school classes and cafeteria were on the first floor and the high school classes were upstairs on 2nd floor. Individual classes varied in size from 3 -10 students per class year. (approx. 100 students in 12 grades) As a result, several grades were grouped together in one room. Miss Carolyn Prater was my first grade teacher. My 2nd grade teacher was Miss Theresa Haughton. 3rd, 4th and 5th grade were taught together in another room with Mrs. Naomi Presnell and Mrs. Lena Curry as teachers. We sat on benches at the front of the room for the class discussions.

Art & Charlotte, 2006

We read out loud or did math problems on the board. In 3rd & 4th grade, I often listened to the reading classes for upper grades while I was doing other school work. I don't know how many Bobbsey Twins, Nancy Drew, Mark Twain, particularly Tom Sawyer and Huck Finn stories the teacher read after lunch but we all thought they were a great diversion. Mrs. Opal Sisley was my teacher in 6th, 7th & 8th grade.

1954 Girls Basketball Team

During my high school years, I had one teacher who inspired me and all of my classmates more than any other in our small classes. Leo Rieman (See separate attached tribute) wore many hats, he served as Superintendent, as well as the math, history and science teacher. He motivated us to be the best we could be. His history classes broadened our scope of the world.

Mr. Rieman is the one teacher that my husband and I visited whenever we returned to the area for vacations.

Dad was elected to the school board when I was in high school. In fact, he presented my high school diploma to me in the new gym, now a community center. The Idaho State Board of Education was encouraging the consolidation of rural schools about that time.

After a couple trips to Boise to learn what the options were, dad and other school board members learned that the Reubens and Winchester school districts would be consolidated about 1953. They maintained separate schools, with one school board for both schools. When these two schools were consolidated with Craigmont in 1962, the Winchester school and Reubens school were closed.

As I look back on those high school years in a small school environment, I have to say there are many memories. More students had the opportunity to hone their leadership and organizational skills because there weren't many of us to take the responsibility of doing things. I worked on the school newspaper and the yearbook staff. I was in several high school plays, played the role of Aunt Letty in our Class play.

My sport was girls' basketball when the girls played on one half of the court. I played the forward position on the girl's team and lettered every year for four years. At that time, they believed that it was better to have women play on half the court, not so strenuous!

Art, Clarice and Charlotte

I was a majorette with the band for four years in high school. We marched with the band during special parades at the Lewis and NezPerce County fairs and other events. We performed a twirling routine during half time at the home basketball games. I was a cheerleader for three years. I was a class officer and student body officer as well.

I enrolled at the University of Idaho in the fall of 1955. I majored in pre-nursing for two years. In my junior year I switched my major to psychology and I received my B.S degree in Psychology in 1959. This background has served me well throughout my life as I have had to interact with various cultures in different countries where we lived as a family.

Charlotte's Tribute to Leo Rieman

"A Person Who Inspired Me"

A person, who has inspired me, besides my parents, was a special high school teacher we had in our small rural high school in Northern Idaho. During my high school years, Leo Rieman inspired me and all of my classmates more than any other in our small classes. He wore many hats; he served as Superintendent, as well as the math, history/geography and science teacher.

He motivated us to be the best we could be. His history classes broadened our scope of the world. When I saw the Taj Mahal, in India, for the first time, I remembered him telling the Richard Halliburton travel story of swimming in the fountains on the Taj Mahal grounds in India.

He was able to capture historical events and whet your appetite to learn everything you could about other parts of the world. He is probably one of the reasons my husband ended up with an international career that allowed us to live and travel in countries around the world. Mr. Rieman brought an enthusiasm to learning that made him a unique educator.

To his credit, his students became a renowned nuclear physicist, engineers, the first woman Accounting/CPA grad at the U of I, International business executives, CPA firm owners, agricultural experts, many distinguished educators, nurses and outstanding farmers. Mr. Rieman is the one teacher that my husband and I visited whenever we returned to north Idaho for vacations. He has passed away but we still see his 90+ yr. wife at school reunions.

At a recent school reunion, honoring Mr. Rieman and his wife, several stories were told about him. Even though Mr. Rieman could have gone to a larger school district, he chose to return to the Camas prairie area where he had grown up. I remember, he motivated by example. He was always dressed in a suit and tie.

You didn't want to be called to his office for a talk! He didn't raise his voice but very calmly had heart to heart talks with some of the guys in his office when they had skipped class, gone off campus, were caught smoking or whatever. A call to his office could mean extra study halls, ineligibility to play basketball, depending on the circumstances. These infractions seem simple compared to the issues teachers deal with on a daily basis now.

An example of his dedication was a story that was not well known at the time. A high school student, one of my neighbors, was diagnosed with TB and confined to bed rest for some months. Gary, a brilliant student, couldn't go to class so Mr. Rieman visited Gary at home and tutored him in all subjects, plus advanced math & calculus, that weren't on regular curriculum.

Gary Dau went on to get his PhD in nuclear physics and worked at the Hanford Reactor and with the Atomic Energy Department in Palo Alto, CA before he passed away from cancer in his mid-fifties. This is just one example of how we all benefited from Mr. Rieman's inspiration.

Because Mr. Rieman cared deeply about the school and educational community, he worked closely with my dad, who was on the school board, to help float a bond to fund two gymnasiums/multipurpose buildings in the newly consolidated school district. They are now community buildings because another school consolidation happened in mid-sixties.

He had varied interests. He co-authored a book, called the "MULLAN ROAD"- published in 1968, that tells about the man and the road in northern Idaho (now Interstate 90) that was named after Captain Mullan. We have a couple of copies, now out of print, of this book. As a matter of interest, I did a search on the book and found it available for $100+ on one website that handles sales of old books.

Another hobby he had was being a "rock hound". He and his brother accumulated quite a collection of rocks and special stones during their treks in the mountains of Idaho. We visited them, during our home leaves, after he retired. I remember our young daughters were fascinated by the polished stones, of all types that he had. In particular, he had a large collection of garnets, which are readily available in north central Idaho if you know where to "pan" for them.

I think one of the things that made the Riemans very special was that they looked upon their students as extended family. One time, Mrs. Rieman said to me that Mr. Rieman was always very proud to hear of the accomplishments of his students. We all should have a Mr. Rieman in tour lives.

2011: Charlotte Ruckman Misner

Donna Mae Leeper Huntley

Spouse: Les Huntley

I attended Reubens school all 12 years. Someone else in my class told who the teachers were; I believe it was Charlotte. Fred O'Brien, Charlotte Ruckman, Jim Brackett and I were together the whole time. I think Don Hill joined us about 3rd grade and he also was always in school those years. We had others come and go through the years.

I got very good grades except in conduct. I now have a little granddaughter in Texas who is much like I was. Just cannot keep her hands to herself. I think it was in 1st grade that I came back from the bathroom and saw everyone had their heads down on their desk resting. I clunked everyone in the whole row on the head with my knuckles as I went back to my seat. I don't remember what my punishment was.

I loved Tressa Haughton and I thought she was the tallest lady in the world. In 4th grade we had Mrs. Curry. She was my toughest teacher. I spent a lot of time in the library which was basically a closet. The ceiling was 10 feet high and there was a window high up so it was not dark but I would get a book and read until I heard her coming back and then I put it away.

One day I waved when the train went by and Mrs. Curry made me stand at the window and wave for what seemed forever. Since I got good grades I finished my work quickly and then got into mischief. Once I was throwing my hankie up in the air and catching it so I had to stand in front of the whole room and do that forever also.

I loved school and would always get there by the time the doors opened and would help whoever I could. Fred was my best friend as our families were together a lot. I remember one day Gregory Nelson who lived with Boyers did something to me and I can still see Fred chasing him around the school house. I don't know if he caught him or not.

On recess we would get the high school boys to push us in the swings as they were so tall. I especially remember Bud Chambers pushing me until I thought I would wrap around the pole at the top. That was one of the advantages of all ages in the same building. We would play fox and geese in the snow but I think that was just with kids our own age.

I know several people have mentioned when Kenneth Simmons fell through the heater grate . It was on the 2nd floor and he fell clear to the basement. I was in grade school but I saw him when he came up the stairs and he was all beat up.

Mr. Rieman was a good principal and teacher. He didn't stand for any nonsense either. He usually went home around 4 p.m. One day Lorraine Becker and I climbed the ladder into the bell tower. Probably Charlotte would have been with us too but she had to catch the bus.

Donna with Princesses Charlotte & Henrietta

The ladder was right by Mr. Rieman's office. That day he did not go home at 4 as I am sure he knew we were up there. It was great fun for awhile but by the time 5 o'clock came it wasn't fun anymore and we could not come down until he left. I am sure I got in trouble at home for being so late.

In those days if kids got in trouble at school they also were in trouble at home. That was a good thing as we thought twice before we did something wrong-- or most people did.

I got good grades but could not get algebra

through my head. Mr. Rieman knew it so well he just could not get it through my head either. Fred finally tutored me and it made sense then.

GAA Officers 1955

I was born on May 1st and my dad teased me by telling me I came in a May basket and it was left on the door step so they couldn't take me back. My sister was 4 and a half years older and when I got to be 5 or 6 I became my dad's boy. Everta helped in the house and I helped outside. I learned to milk when I was about ten, and feed the pigs and chickens and do all the outside chores.

(The following is adapted from a 2009 Lewiston Tribune article) *I practically grew up in a grain elevator. My dad, Vinal Leeper, managed the Lewiston Grain Growers elevators in Reubens for 25 years. They built a new elevator of 2 by 10 or 2 by12 planks laid flat and spiked together in 1947 when I was 10. It was about 100 feet high and is still in use today.*

Annual Staff 1954

The workers would set me on a board and pull me up the outside of that building by block and tackle like I was sitting in a swing. Daddy was afraid of heights and I'm surprised he allowed that.

Once when I was about nine years old my sister and I decided to ride the man lift, a rope and pulley platform elevator for getting to the top floors without climbing ladders. A man lift uses counterweights to balance out the weight on the platform. With the proper counterweight, the platform moves up and down requiring almost no pulling on the rope.

Well, of course, this man lift was set up for my Dad to use, so the counterweight was as heavy as he was. When we stepped on the platform and cut it loose, it shot us clear up to the top of the elevator. The two of us were not any where near as heavy as our Dad and weren't strong enough to pull that weight up so we couldn't get down. Daddy had to climb the ladder and bring us down. He was terribly afraid of heights so that was a real sacrifice for him to do that.

Those were great days. We knew all the farmers who brought grain in. When I was 14, Daddy had a small stroke during harvest and they needed a substitute. Daddy convinced the head office that I knew the business and could weigh and unload trucks better than anybody. So they hired me. That would be unheard of nowadays and maybe against the law.

I used to play on stacks of sacked gain in the flat house or boxcars they were loading. Once I fell asleep in a car and they shut the door and hooked it onto the train. I woke up screaming and they opened the car before it got very far.)

Reubens was a railroad town and the tracks split the town in two. We lived on the north side, the "wrong" side of the tracks. We used to walk down the railroad track to the tunnels and go through a few. I don't remember if we started from home or maybe someone took us to Chesley. Also I could walk from the railroad crossing near the warehouse to school on the rail without falling off. Not every time but many times.

I went fishing and hunting often with my dad and Bill Thomason and sometimes Ray O'Brien and Fred.

My cousin Genevieve Simmons attended school at RHS and I believe she graduated despite having a brain and spinal tumor. She was in a bed or a wheelchair for a few years and I would go over and entertain her and play a board game or something. I think that was the start of my wanting to be a nurse. She passed away at a young age, in her 20s as I remember.

I am having a good life. I married Les Huntley in 1960 and we have 4 children, 10 grands 5 greats and a grand and a great waiting for us in Heaven. What fun they all are. We have been married 54 years and counting.

We moved to Boulder, Colorado in 1960. In 1968, after I had the three older children in one school, I went to nurses training and got my LPN. I loved being a nurse. I worked in a hospital for 4 years in Boulder, then when we spent 6 years in the Craigmont area I worked in both Cottonwood and Grangeville hospitals and for Dr. Imhoff in his clinic

When we moved to Seattle area I drove school bus a couple of years for a Christian school and then created a job for myself in a medical clinic and worked there for 15 years. It was a great experience. Now I volunteer at St. Joseph Hospital here in Lewiston so I can be close to the medical field.

50th Anniversary

Les traveled a lot in his job as a metrologist (measurement scientist) for the National Bureau of Standards in Boulder Colorado and later for Fluke in Everett, Washington. My mother lived with us for a few years in Boulder and that gave me opportunity to travel with Les sometimes. I have been in England, Germany, Holland Singapore, Korea, Malaysia Chile, Argentina, Hawaii, Mexico, Hondurus, Belieze, The Bahamas and China. Probably have missed some; I know I left out Canada.

We retired back to Idaho in 1995 and spent 10 months traveling with our fifth wheel before settling into our home here in Lewiston. We have traveled much with RV's, have been to all 50 states and are still traveling. We've spent many months in Texas where our daughter Dreena

Our Family, March, 2010
Darinda, Jason, Les, Me, Dreena, Guy

lives with Paul and their five adopted children. We try to spend every Halloween and Thanksgiving with them.

We have a great church family and Pastor in Emmanuel Baptist Church. I help in the nursery and office occasionally. We helped start an exercise class for seniors and led it at times until creaky joints put an end to that. Currently I am in charge of our email prayer chain.

Andy Rooney said:, *"I've learned that I can always pray for someone when I don't have the strength to help him in some other way."*

Doran Rogers

Spouse: Sandy Rogers

DREAMS DO STILL COME TRUE

Moving to the country near Melrose was an experience in itself. I started the 4th grade at Reubens and my first teacher was Mrs. Curry. One thing I remember about her was that she didn't like us looking out the window watching the steam engines at the Reubens Depot.

The small gym at Reubens holds a lot of memories because of all the basketball games, plays and especially the "Foxy Grandma", play in which I played, you guessed it, Foxy Grandma. Mrs. Hays was an excellent teacher and director of the plays.

In High School I remember my favorite teacher was Principal, Leo Rieman, he really had a heart for the school and was a nice guy. In the summer between my Junior and Senior year I grew 5 inches and surprised some people. Some of us boys would tell Mr. Rieman that we had to go home and help with the farm work. As I remember, we would get out at about 2:00pm and go down to the trestles to shoot squirrels. It worked out pretty good until he figured out what we were up to.

I graduated in 1955 and went to work for General Tire. In 1959 I was married with a 6 month old daughter and we moved to Englewood, California. I went to school at the Northrup Institute of Technology and one year later received my Airframe and Power Plant License from the FAA. I then worked for United Airlines as a jet engine mechanic and thought about going into their program for pilot training with the goal of flying for them.

But, as the saying goes, I couldn't get the farm out of the boy, so we moved back home in 1961 and I went to work for Hillcrest Aircraft and later for Arrow Aviation located on the Lewiston Airport.

A big change came when I started Cascade Flying Service in 1966, crop dusting in Royal City, then Othello and the Palouse area in Garfield, Washington. We repaired damaged Ag aircraft in the winter to support my flying habit. During this time we built a paved airstrip, a large shop to hold 4 airplanes, other hangers and a new home by 1975.

We made too many trips cross country to count with our 1 ton truck and trailer, buying damaged aircraft to rebuild. We always got a lot of comments along the road such as, "Oh he wrecked his airplane", "Is that a wrecked airplane?" Sandy would quietly say, "Oh Duh".

At one time we thought we would count the airplanes but realized it was too many to remember. I retired from Ag flying after 37 years and sold the business to another crop duster after 40 years of operation.

In 1998 due to the unreliability of the old radial engines, forced landings due to engine failure and other problems, I started looking for a different power plant. Due to the Soviet Union meltdown, aircraft and engines became available in the Czech Republic. After talking to the owners of the Walter Company in the Czech Republic, I took both my sons-in-law and went to Prague.

We were able to pen a deal with them to purchase the 751horsepower Walter turbine engines from them and install them on the Ag aircraft we had received an STC from the FAA. We have 7 STC's and a PMA from the FAA which allows us to put the engines on the aircraft we have rebuilt or on customer aircraft or to be able to send them out as kits.

In 2013 we signed a contract with Pratt & Whitney (the largest aircraft engine company in the world) to sell and install their new and overhauled PT6 engines. We again had to get FAA approval and are in the process of doing the flight testing. We are excited to see where this new chapter leads us.

Because of the interest and sales for our conversion, we have traveled to Australia, Canada, Brazil, Costa Rica, Guatemala, Argentina, Uruguay, South Africa and the Czech Republic.

Married for 47 years Sandy and I have 3 girls, 6 grand children and 3 great grandchildren. We sold our home in Garfield to our General Manager and built a home at the top of the old Spiral Highway. Doran pretends to be retired but still goes up to the shop three days a week and is on the phone often.

At this time I must honor my Lord and Savior Jesus Christ for all the blessings and favor he has given me throughout my life. What an adventure it has been!

Fred O'Brien

Spouse: Elzo O'Brien

I attended all 12 years of my schooling at Reubens, Idaho, graduating from high school in 1955. Remembering details of the eight years I spent in grade school is rather difficult, so most of my discussion will concern my high school years with an occasional reference to the earlier years.

In 1951, I entered high school at Reubens joined by six other members of my class: Donna Leeper, Charlotte Ruckman, Jim Brackett, Doran Rogers, Richard Becker, and Don Hill. It was an unusual class in that we all managed to graduate together with no additions or deletions from our class during that period. We do still see each other occasionally, especially at reunion events. I value their friendship.

The drafty old two-story building that contained the Reubens School remains a clear memory of mine. The floors were bare wood with no paint that I can remember no carpet, no tile, just plain old wood. Although today's populace seems to think all facilities should be brand new with the very finest of everything, our drafty, old wooden floored building still provided a place where a student could receive a good education.

For some reason, these fancy facilities don't seem to advance our educational progress in the state of Idaho. In spite of the austere facilities in the Reubens School, my background there gave me the foundation to handle well the curriculum at the University of Idaho. In fact, I managed to achieve the second highest grade point in my living group the first semester. I say this not to brag, but to make the point that our simple school provided an excellent basis for future schooling.

Fred Self Portrait

Leo Reiman was our superintendent, principal, teacher, disciplinarian, and encourager. He would start every morning in the high school study hall reading the Scripture to the four grades gathered there. We had to be quiet, make no comment or have any discussion about the reading.

It didn't seem to hurt us and may have done us some good. It seems a real shame that our society has gone the direction it has. That is where I received my first Bible, probably during a school assembly presented by the Gideons.

A few words would be in order about Mr. Rieman. A man who held my deepest respect, he was always fair in his discipline and in his classes. I found his classes to be particularly fascinating and interesting. Some of his history stories may have been beyond the pale, but we certainly learned the points he wanted to make.

I heard him many times say when we weren't performing during the class that perhaps we should drop out of school, acquire 40 acres and a mule (insinuating that we should get an education). He would not allow any of his students to say that something could not be done. We could not use the word can't in his class.

Grandpa O'Briens '26 Dodge, 1953

He was extremely fair when it came to discipline. I used to be called into his office when he was investigating some horrendous deed performed by one or more of his students. He would ask me if I was involved, and if I said "yes", he would say, "don't do it anymore". If I said "no", he would ask if I knew who did the deed. If I did know who did it, I would say "yes, I did know who did it, but I'm not going to tell you who did it".

With that, he would thank me and send me back to class. There was no pressure to "rat" on my friends. He was also a man of wisdom. I could have graduated in three years by picking up one extra class (my sister had done that). when I went to talk to him about this possibility he said, "No, you need another year of maturity before you start to college". He was certainly right.

Fred's Mom in the snow, 1955

Reubens had 25 students and five teachers. Today's teachers would be "green with envy" over this student ratio. We were very fortunate.

All students had the opportunity to participate in sports (basketball and boxing), music, school politics, drama, dances, and other activities. Every student was an officer of something and had the opportunity to develop speaking, organizing, and planning skills. Because of this, many learned life-long skills. I, for one, learned to stand before a group and talk. This was a lifelong advantage given to me by this small school.

Kathy Elzo Tamara Steve David

The one and only trophy in our trophy case was a good sportsmanship trophy won by some prior class. We never won any district tournaments or championships, but we were still champions. There were always small victories individually and as a team such as beating Lewiston "B" team three times in a row with them sending a little better team each time we played them.

Participating in our small band enabled us to learn the skill of reading music. I am amazed today at how few individuals know how to read music. We worked as a team putting together the school newspaper, and also the yearly annual. This teamwork extended to many other activities such as organizing dances, and so on.

Our class was extremely ambitious when it came to raising money. We volunteered for any project that would turn a dollar for our class of '55. When it came time for our annual sneak at the end of the year we had a huge war chest of money and we were able to take a trip to Portland, where we attended the horse races (our long shot came in dead last), and the follies. We also spent time in the costal town of Seaside, Oregon, before returning home. It was a senior sneak to truly remember.

Kevin's Wedding

Another advantage of the small town and school is that we were allowed to go downtown to the store where the school bus would pick us up and take us home. You would not likely see this happening in today's society.

One drawback from a small school and community was that, if you screwed up, Mom got the word before you arrived home. We had a rather lively evening one winter night playing tag with our cars. Whoever was "it" had to come up behind another car, bump their bumper, and then they would be "it". Roads were very slick and it was really fun.

We even broke in the newly planted city park. I don't believe we missed driving over a single tree in the park that night. Amazingly, we apparently didn't kill any trees. The game ended when one of the participants tried to get away by going up the railroad tracks. We were sure concerned that a train might come by while we were trying to get that car off the tracks. This was one of the events that Mom knew all about when I got home that night.

I wouldn't trade my time and education at Reubens for any other school in the world. I am truly blessed to be an alumnus of the Reubens High School and would like to give thanks for the teachers and staff who herded us through our formative years.

Class of 1956

Lawrence Courtney

Spouse: Rita Courtney

I attended school at Reubens: I started school at Reubens in the fall of 1947. I was in the fourth grade and transferred from Peck, 1D. I spent the rest of my schooling at Reubens and graduated May of 1956. When I started: in the fourth grade there was Lorraine Becker, Gary Dau and myself. As I remember it the 5th grade was when they closed the school in Gifford and Jeannette Stolte joined our class.

I remember that Lena Curry was our teacher through the 5th Grade. I do remember how some of the students would bring a bunch of peanuts to school and we'd give our teacher a peanut shower. Then everyone jumped in and helped clean up all the peanuts.

Opal Sisley was our teacher for the 6th and 7th grade years. Patricia Cole was our teacher for the 8th grade year. She was a rather new teacher and tried to be rather strict with us. We'd gotten our heads together and planned a Peanut Shower for her.

One of the girls had been helping in the lunch room and when she returned to the class-room she informed Mrs. Cole that Alice Stauty-wanted to see her: While she went to see Alice the peanuts were distributed and someone knocked on the door that was between our classroom and the lunch-room.

That was the signal to Alice that we were ready for our teacher to return. When Mrs. Cole got to the front of the room she started to scold us for not being quiet. That was when the Peanut Shower began. Oh, but she didn't know what to think at first but turned out to be a good sport. Alice told us later when the knock on the door signal came that Mrs Cole said "I told them kids to be quiet."

I am not sure when Paul Creswell joined us, but I remember Lorraine Dehning joining us either in 8th grade or Freshman year. Gary Dau became ill and was in Spokane and was at Edgewood as I remember and I got to go to Spokane with his father,, George Dau to visit. Gary then got to return home and Mr. Rieman would go out to their place and give Gary his assignments.

By Mr. Rieman doing this Gary was able to maintain all of his studies. I doubt that something like that would take place in this day and age. The mighty class of five graduated in 1956.

"Forward ever, never backward, for within ourselves our future lies." Lorraine Becker, Lorralne Dehninq , JeannetteStolte,

Gary Dau and I finished our education at RHS. I haven't seen Lorrairie Dehning since Commencement exercises.

Reubens was blessed with Richard Scott being the coach and teacher for the school years of 52 to 56. He really brought the basketball teams along and made them great contenders.

Special school memories during my time at Reubens: One special memory that I will note is how wonderful it was that the School Districts were able to build the new Gyms in Reubens and Winchester.

I am grateful for: All the support that the community gave the School and always attended all of the school functions. It took everybody to make events successfully and I can't remember any failures.

Comments: I have been able to return for the Reubens Community Sausage Feed a few times. I also have returned to pay final tribute to several members of the community.

I've always counted my blessing for being raised on a farm and going to school at Reubens.

CLASS OF 1957

Larry L. Curry

Spouse: Ann (Knowlton) Curry

I attended school at Reubens from 1945-1957, grades 1-12.

Special school memories during my time at Reubens:

Basketball games in which I was a participant,

Playground activities with classmates,

Sneaking off the school ground to the forbidden Old Barrow Pit,

School dances,

School plays,

Band trips,

Picnics at Craig Junction and

The closeness to classmates that only come from a small school environment. Everyone was included in activities, unique to small schools. Everyone supported one another.

I am grateful for the opportunity to have grown up and been educated in a small school environment. We received lots of individual attention from our teachers and received a good, basic education.

Special thanks to those who give their time and support to see that the yearly reunion takes place.

Ronald Stellyes

Spouse Duthiel Stellyes

Ron & Duthiel, 2006

I attended Reubens School all 12 years of my education. I started in 1st grade in 1945 and graduated in 1957.

Mr. Rieman came to Reubens the year we started 1st grade and stayed until we graduated. If we were quiet in study hall he would let us listen to the World Series. Mrs. Curry (Lena) was our teacher for 3rd–5th grades and would read to us everyday after lunch. Joe Decicio and I cleaned the school every night during 7th and 8th grades. We each received 25¢ and a candy bar every night for our work.

Ron and Joyce Stellyes 1955

In high school, we would sneak out of school early and go squirrel hunting. One winter everyone on the bus had to spend the night at Ray and Marie O'Brien's because of a snowstorm.

Ron's Car 1.5 Miles N. of Reubens, March 1966
Jim McCall, Earnest Stellyes, Ron Stellyes

My three oldest daughters attended Reubens school until it closed. My parents were the janitors at the school until it closed.

CLASS OF 1959

Ann Knowlton Curry

Spouse: Larry Curry

I attended school at Reubens from 1947 to 1959. I began the first grade in Reubens the year the "Melrose Kids" went to Reubens. I met Mrs. Skeels, my first grade teacher, before school started but I didn't know any of the kids. I remember some snickers.

The long 3–5 grade years could never be forgotten; the joy of the playground and the Valentine parties. Sixth grade was a new age–the male teachers were veterans and such permissiveness and new ways of learning were fun.

High school seemed to revolve around basketball games and cheerleading. It seemed to last forever; new teachers spiced it up. Our big class of 7 graduated in 1959; which according to one author was the year that changed the world.

Some of my most vivid memories are the school bus rides and the winters of 1947 and 1948. These winters the snow was so deep that going to school was risky. I remember not being able to keep up as we all walked in to school after getting stuck a ways out of Reubens.

Indelible memories are the times we got stranded for several days at other peoples' homes; one time at the Courtneys' and once at the Currys'. Evie Curry made me a circular skirt and you could roller skate in their house. My most enduring memories are of creating games and role-playing on the playground– venturing to the very boundary. And other times, playing on the big swings and the now banned giant strides. I loved school and looked forward to every day. I always remember being treated with patience and respect.

I am grateful for not having to make choices; certain things were givens, like where you went to school. I think it was an idyllic time and place. We were all taking the same subjects; we didn't choose friends; they were our classmates. We all watched the same TV shows and talked about them. Our parents were mostly farmers; we didn't know rich or poor. We were blissfully homogeneous.

I'm not in favor of such small schools. I think they limit the student for his future. It is good to have a long history of people who know you and are still your friends!

Loretta Skelton Stevens

Spouse: Mike Stevens

Memories of Reubens School days:

We all wanted to ring the school bell and sometimes Mr. Marquam would let us. When we pulled the bell rope, it would pull us up in the air. So much fun, we thought.

I remember the old kitchen where we had to get our shots.

Loretta & Mike

The fun we had playing softball with the boys.

The Sadie Hawkins dance. Some of us girls got tipsy and Mr. Reiman "let us have it" the next day at school. I was dishing up the potato salad, but was missing the plates. Not good.

I remember our Christmas plays, how much hard work, but so much fun. We got out of class to rehearse.

I loved Mrs. Curry, once I got over being scared of her. She read to us every day and took us to other places; I even have some of the Reubens Library books my kids brought home from their school in Craigmont. I treasure them.

I loved marching in the parades. I usually got a blister on my heel, but it was fun.

Also, I loved being a cheerleader and cheering for the boys. My brother Billie played basketball. I surely miss him.

I remember skipping school one day to go to Lewiston with a bunch of friends. Boy did I get in trouble, especially with my Mom.

One time I also got kicked out of school because I signed out to go to town. Some other kids met me over the hill and went with me. We all got in a lot of trouble. Now look how many kids leave the school grounds at noon.

Gary Willson

Spouse: Janell Dufour Willson

Gary Willson graduated from Reubens High School in 1959. He attended school there for 1 year. Because of a serious illness when he was in the first grade, he had to stay at home and his mother, Cappie, was his teacher that first year.

He married Janell Dufour on May 21, 1966. She was raised in Culdesac and the daughter of Art and Eileen Dufour. Gary and Janell have farmed and ranched in the Reubens area for 47 years. They have raised three daughters on the farm and their grandson, Willson Lowe, is the 5th generation to farm the land.

Their youngest daughter, Debbie Lowe, is married to Luke Lowe and they farm and raise cattle in Reubens. They have two children, Willson who is 20 and Chantell who is 18. Luke is also the Mayor of Reubens.

DeDe Goeckner is married to Andy Goeckner and they farm and raise Hereford cattle on the brakes of the Salmon River south of Craigmont. They have three children, Tanner 16, Katie 9 and Ty 7.

Joy Beckman is married to Warren Beckman and they

both teach school in Lewiston. Warren teaches at Camelot school and Joy has taught English at Jennifer Junior High for 21 years. In 2012, Joy was chosen Teacher of the Year in the Lewiston School District. Their children are Garrett 13 and Gabe 10.

Gary has lived in Reubens all his life. It's a great place to live and raise a family. In 2004 Gary and Janell traveled to Baja, Mexico to check it out. They now spend the winter months there, returning in the spring to help Luke and Willson with the farming.

Patsy Symmes Gjendem.

I moved to Reubens when I was three years old and attended all 12 grades at the Reubens School graduating in May of 1959. Growing up in Reubens,

I remember:

When Margaret Meacham was the telephone operator and then Dorothy Scott became the operator.

When I found Wonder Bread wax paper wrappers neatly folded in a cupboard at Aunt Allie's home.

When my Dad was Santa at the Christmas program in the old gym I saw him changing out of Santa suit in the kitchen and ran into the gym yelling "My Daddy's Santa Claus."

Barney, Dave, Patsy, Barbara, and Tom

There were coal cinders from the school furnace spread on part of the school playground. Some of them ended up in my knees!

Evelyn Crow teaching 4-H cooking and sewing classes at her home.

Going to Craigmont to get Carnival supplies with Gordon Laird, Larry Curry and Ann Knowlton and hitting a pheasant so we picked it up, brought it to my home, cooked it and ate it.

Loretta Skelton and Patsy reading names on headstones in the Reubens cemetery in the summer.

Walking around the Big Block from home to Bill Scott's then Rob Scott's, to the school and home.

When June Meacham, Loretta and Patsy were little girls living on the same street.

Going to Christmas and Thanksgiving dinner at Grandma and Grandpa's with the family.

When Andy Becker supervised the new addition at the Reubens Church.

When a shepherd came walking through Reubens with a herd of sheep. He gave me a tiny lamb; it was sick and didn't live long.

The March birthday party our parents gave us when Ronnie, Peggy, Gary, Ann and Patsy turned 16.

When Mrs. O'Brien first came to Reubens to teach school; I was in 6th grade.

Most people in town called Adelia Shaul "Aunt Dea". When I was young I took pride in the fact that Aunt Dea was my real aunt!!

Riding bikes with Lorraine Becker and picking delicious yellow plums growing in a fence row.

Loretta and Patsy washing dishes and cleaning house at Mr. and Mrs. Phillips' home.

When the Misner family moved away from Reubens to Eugene, Oregon.

When the Frank West family moved into the Misner home next door to our house.

Randy Webb and Patsy trying to ski down a slight hill in Randy's back yard

When our new born calf kicked me and stunned me; didn't know a tiny calf could kick so hard.

Mrs. Skeels was my first grade teacher.

When Carolyn Webb stayed with us in her senior year; I loved having a "big sister"

When Dad cut down the huge Cottonwood tree in our front yard.

When Ralph Becker told me that Santa Claus was not real; we were walking from school toward Bob and Velma Denny's home.

Riding in the bulk tank on the combine during harvest in the days before the combines had levelers.

My baby sister was a cute baby and that it was fun to have a little sister.
My brother wanted "to be a farmer just like my Dad".

Mr. Prine and his long gray beard and his little house with a wood stove in the living room.

Taking flute lessons from Mr. Davidson and Mom making me practice every day.

Coming home from visiting Grandma Symmes in Spokane and finding Main Street buildings had all burned to the ground.

Lora Skelton's bright red Buick convertible.

A family picnic beside a small creek in Andy Becker's pasture near our farm.

When Joanne, Joyce and Judy Scott were little girls who lived across the street.

When Birdie and Francie West lived next door. What a blessing they were and also like big sisters.

That Betty Brackett was my Sunday School teacher for several years.

Playing baseball in the road in front of our house with Lanny Gill and other neighborhood kids.

When Laurine Skelton was Drum Majorette.

When Reubens had a grocery store and post office and Mrs. Denny was the postmistress.

When Alma and Arlo Denny lived next door on the right hand side and I ate a cucumber from her Garden AND she saw me take it AND she was not happy with me.

When Mr. Cannon delivered milk to our house. Sometimes in the winter it would freeze and cause the cream to rise up out of the milk bottle.

When Ann Knowlton joined our first grade class.

When Glen Cannon worked at the seedhouse.

That when Cappie Willson subbed as a teacher she wouldn't allow anyone to say "shut up". Not a Bad thing. Good for Mrs. Willson!

My favorite song to sing in Mrs. Curry's room was "Coming In On A Wing And A Prayer".

My parents went shopping in Lewiston and were late getting home so I started milking Molly the cow. I took too long and she lay down and Kenny Patton came to my rescue and finished milking.

That Loretta and Patsy were candle lighters at Francie and Keith's wedding and that we had pretty Blue dresses.

When Denny Dau had to recite "Trees" by Joyce Kilmore in Jr. high.

Eating "Charlie Brackett Beefsteak" at the Brackett's home. It was really liver but I liked it.

Babysitting at Jim and Rosie McCalls.

Elmer Staley driving into Reubens in his black early 1920's Model T Ford.

My Mom giving "shots" and first aid to Reubens townspeople and wanting "shots" too.

At this writing it has been 54 years since I graduated from Reubens. It has been interesting reminiscing about growing up in Reubens, Idaho. It was good to have grown up in Reubens.

CLASS OF 1960

Eileen Stauty Brackett

Spouse: Jim Brackett

Halloween night was always special in Reubens. Each year someone would try to come up with something more exciting than the previous year. Lewiston Grain Growers used to put their pea screenings in burlap bags, piling the bags in long rows outside. "The Group" decided it would be fun to haul a bunch of the screenings to the school and block all the doors. It took a lot of trips, but finally all the doors were piled high and deep.

When we arrived at school the next morning someone had moved just enough bags by the front door so we could get in. The rest of the doors were still blocked.

Mr. Gould, who was our Principal at the time, called us all into the study hall. He said it looked like some people had worked really hard last night. He said he didn't have any idea who had put the screenings by the doors, but he needed the bags hauled back to Lewiston Grain Growers. He looked at all of us and said, "Would you, you, you and you please do that for me?"

Jim Brackett - 1955

It was as if he had watched the whole thing happen. What could they say? They got to handle those screenings again. I bet he was smiling all the way back to his office. He got the last laugh.

Dennis Decicio

Spouse: Connie Decicio

Memories of Reubens School Days

I was born in Lewiston Idaho in 1941. My father, Forch Decicio, worked for the Camas Prairie Railroad. We moved to Reubens from Lenore Idaho in May of 1945. One of my few memories of that time was we had to walk across the bridge over the Clearwater River on a plank as the bridge deck was being repaired. The people were talking about the war in Europe ending. Dad was the section forman for the Camas Prairie Railroad.

I started school in 1947. Spent 2 wonderful years in the second grade and somehow kept myself out of trouble until I graduated from high school in May 1960. I was sometimes referred to as one of those *xo# Decicio kids or that sweet little Decicio boy, depending on the particular occasion.

I wasn't a very good student as I didn't really like school very much. I would always get to school early so I could play on the swing sets. And that was about the extent of my enthusiasm for school. In the fifth grade we learned how to play a musical instrument, the tonette. I also learned what it was like to have a crush on Mrs. Hayes.

Dennis 8 months

The next year most of us began playing in the school band. Because my parents couldn't afford a new horn, I was given an old E-flat tuba to play. The next year the school bought a used B- flat sousaphone that I was told if I put so much as one dent in it, it would be off with my head. That horn and I got along reasonably well the next five years.

I think the deck was stacked in my favor when I was selected to be a part of the All North Western Band Conference in Seattle in my junior year. In sports I played basketball which I didn't get along with reasonably well. My only claim to fame was playing baseball. I broke up a no hitter against Culdesac in the top of the sixth inning with a line drive up the middle.

At one time there were six of us in our class. Most of us were together from the fifth grade on. Eileen Stauty, Billie Skelton, John Watson and I managed to hang in there to the bitter end. I can honestly say that I graduated fourth in my class.

One of the things I remember was the time Tommy Hudson and I took a hard right turn on our way to school one fine spring morning. We found our way to the bottom of Lapwai canyon to fish a little. My mother was waiting for me when I got home. Can't get away with anything in a small town! During play practice in high school, John Watson and I were shooting ground squirrels out the back window of the gym.

I remember the deep snow in the winter of 1948-1949. Dad and the section crew left with the train to help clear the tracks to Grangeville. They got stuck in a cut just south of Ferdinand for over two weeks. Dad said they would just about get the steam engine dug out before it would blow shut again. He and his crew walked home from Craigmont with a sled loaded with food.

In Reubens we were snowed in for over two weeks. I remember someone dropping boxes of bread and oatmeal from a red airplane, and I remember not being too impressed with the oatmeal. I also remember little piles of snow on the living room floor that blew in during the night that year. It wasn't until just a few years ago that I realized my mother took care of us three boys' and my little sister who was only nine months old alone during that time. I have all the respect in the world for her.

I remember the town burning down, in 1952 I think. And I remember waiting not so patiently to grow big enough to get work in the summer that didn't involve picking rocks. At the age of 15 I started working at the seed house doing all the hard work no one else would do. I don't remember how many grain trucks I had to unload with nothing more than a shovel. That meant that I didn't have to buck hay bales for farmers whose sons all of a sudden came down with a case of severe hay fever.

Francie says, *"The big fire in Reubens was in 1955. (I have the newspaper article dated July 15, 1955. That was on Friday, the fire started Wednesday night. I'll never forget that night. I had just gone upstairs to my bedroom and saw the flames going up the side of the store. I dashed down to the church and rang the bell as fast as I could—the fire alarm. What a night!")*

One day Eileen and I someone I don't remember found an old wood burning cook stove near my house. We were about 10 or 11 years old. We got the idea to bake some apples. So we all went home to get everything that would be needed. My job was to get the matches to build a fire which wasn't all that easy–It was known that I may have upon occasion, smoked. We succeeded with our task. But it's a wonder we didn't burn the countryside down.

While in grade school, my younger brother, John, found several bottles of beer under the bridge on the road that leads to Eldridge Gills place. Well, John promptly reported it to proper authorities and we promptly took care of the beer. We didn't want the high school boys to get into trouble.

I think the first time we ever heard of drugs was when a State Trooper came to our school my senior year to lecture us about their evils. It's a good thing he didn't lecture us about the evils of alcohol. We were already well schooled on its evils.

Also in our senior year, a few farm animals wandered into the high school study hall one Halloween. Funny how things like that happen that time of year. Another year a large stack of pea straw bales that were out near the four corners, some how moved to the middle of the road blocking the school bus. About the same time of year.

There were many mentors in my life growing up in Reubens. Most of them were men whom I had a lot of respect for, or feared. Mostly feared. But we all learned to stand up for what we believed in. My father passed away in October 1959, my senior year of high school.

My family had to move to Lewiston because we were living in the house owned by the railroad. I didn't want to change schools that close to graduation. Earl and Cappie Willson didn't hesitate to take me in. Their love and support will always be remembered. As I look back on it, most of those men served during WWII. What better mentors to have had.

USN Mid 1960s

For the sake of going on and on, I would like to tell you about one particular man that made a very profound impact on my future life. That man and his wife were Frank and Jessie West. I joined the US Navy right out of high school, and served in the amphibious Navy on board the USS Catamount LSD 17. The only ship in the US Navy named after a tavern and we did our very best to live up to it.

I was some how honorably discharged in March 1964. I went to work at the Potlatch lumber mill and managed to stay out of trouble long enough to meet a beautiful young lady who had been married. She had four children ages 1 to 4 and was divorced by the age of twenty one. We were married in February 1966 in Lewiston Idaho.

We moved to Gold Beach, Oregon where we started going to church in an effort to start off on the right foot. Connie, my wife, had attended church growing up at Orchards Community Church in Lewiston. She had heard that she needed to have a personal relationship with Jesus Christ, but had never made that commitment.

Connie and Dennis Decicio

One month after our wedding she made that decision to give her life to Christ. I came home from work that evening to find my wife had completely changed. I asked her what had happened to her.

And she showed me from the bible that I needed to accept Jesus Christ as my personal savior, which I did.

A few months later we moved back to Lewiston where I went to work at the Potlatch paper mill for the next seven years. We continued to attend Orchards Community Church where we were involved in the youth group ministry as well as in church leadership. The highlight of each year was the annual Missions Conference. And each time our hearts were moved to respond.

Dennis & Connie
At HQ in Chochacamba, Bolivia

On October, 1973 we were challenged by God to apply for the training with New Tribes Mission whose goal was to reach tribal people in very remote regions around the world. We completed three years of training and on April 1977 we were commissioned as ministers with New Tribes Mission.

The service was held at the Orchards Community Church and after the services there stood Frank and Jessie West. I thought I saw a tear falling down Frank's cheek. He placed one of his big work worn hands on my shoulder and looked me in the eye and said that God had laid on his heart to start praying for me when I was about nine or ten years old. Then he said, "Now I know why." What a MENTOR!

We went to the country of Bolivia, South America, where we spent the first year trying to make friendly contact with a group of the hostile Yuqui natives. They lived in what is called the Green Hell of Bolivia; it is dense jungle for several hundred miles. Loggers and oil exploration were coming into contact with these natives and quite often some of them were killed.

Arrival Day, Chimore

Later we moved to the Chimore River and worked with a group of Yuquis who had been befriended in the late sixties. My wife took care of medical and teaching them hygiene and how to bake bread Bolivian style. These people wore no clothing before they came into contact with the outside world.

I took care of the camp which was a seven day a week job. I also taught reading in their language as well as in Spanish. We had to return to the states after Connie had a stroke at the age of 36. But we are so thankful that our Lord allowed us the opportunity to serve Him there.

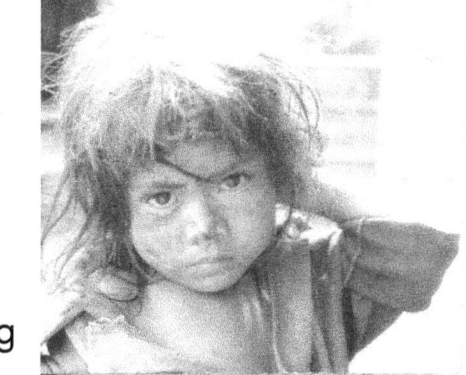

Terista

I hope this will help you. I won't feel bad if you don't use any of this. It's a little bit self incriminating anyway.

I wish all the best, *Dennis Decicio*

CLASS OF 1964

Janice Dau Taft

Spouse: John A Taft

I attended school at Reubens: from 1952 until 1962 when we consolidated with Craigmont and Winchester. My first grade teacher was Mrs. Aletha Pabst who I recently learned is the aunt of Rob Pabst - the husband of my college room mate. There were five classmates that attended all 12 years of school together. We were Janice Dau, John Knowlton, Bob Nichols, Gayle Scott, and Barbara Symmes.

Special school memories during my time at Reubens:

Having small classes

Getting to the school bus around 7:30 and sitting with my friend Linda Hill

Enjoying math and diagramming sentences in grade school

Participating in an end-of-the-school-year picnics where there were lots of fun and food

Watching the freshman wear crazy outfits as part of their initiation into high school

Feeling the rivalry between neighboring towns in basketball and remembering Gerald Woods was our basketball star

Dancing mostly with other girls during the noon break in high school

Participating in community dances and ice-skating parties

Trick or treating at Halloween for coins donated to UNICEF rather than candy

Wearing our coats in high school because the heating system was inadequate

I am grateful for:

Our conservative hometown values

Two parents who raised us five kids and were married over 60+ years

A community where everyone had some connection to farming and understood each others trials and successes

A caring community where individuals volunteered for civic work and were quick to help anyone who was hurt or suffering

I recall an out-of-control fire in the community where the men came and fought the fire and the women brought food to feed the men.

Comments:

Reubens School was small, rural, and not too modern, but it adequately prepared me for college and other pursuits in life. This was certainly true for my brother, Gary, who received his PHD in nuclear engineering.

The Reubens community, in particular, had some wonderful and kind people who readily gave their time to help in community projects and activities.

CLASS OF 1966

Barbara Becker Kotz

Spouse: Alan Kotz

Barbara Becker
First Grade

I attended school at Rebuens; 53-54 school year 54-55 school year 55-56 school year

I remember Mr. Marquam letting us help him ring the school bell. I also remember my 1st grade teacher Mrs. Pabst. She would always bring a small chair and sit by us to help with our school work so she was on our level as she spoke to us. What a wonderful teacher!

L - R: Marilyn Becker, Leona & Tom Armstrong, Barbara & Alan Kotz, Sharon & Ralph Becker, Lorraine Becker

CLASS OF 1969

Jerene Behler Gertonson

Spouse: Pete Gertonson

I went to Reubens School from first grade through fifth, the year Reubens consolidated with Winchester and Craigmont, 1963.

When I was in the second grade, I was coming back from lunch and entering the school from the side door. I was busy with my friends, and when I went to open the door, I didn't notice a dead snake hanging around the door knob. As I reached for the door knob, I touched the snake, and will never forget that feeling! The boys were always catching snakes from the back "playground" and chasing us girls with them.

When I was in the third grade, Mrs. Edelblute was our teacher and we shared a room with the fourth graders. We were sitting in class when all of a sudden plaster from the ceiling fell all over our desks and we looked up and saw the foot of an upper classman. No one was hurt, but it was quite a shock! The school must have been in pretty bad shape then.

Reubens 2nd Grade

I remember playing on the merry-go-round, and to get it going fast, you had to push from the inside. Once, Peggy Zolber was pushing and fell down. Every time she tried to get up her head was hit by the metal bars still moving. Playground equipment had no safety regulations then. I think most every student got hit in the nose with the trick bar. The slide had nails sticking up and it wasn't uncommon to get a sliver in your leg on the way down.

At recess, we played a lot of "Annie Over", soft ball, "Blind Man's Bluff" and "Red Rover". Our teachers were always involved with all activities. I remember one occasion we talked Miss Riggers into riding the merry-go-round. She was so dizzy when she got off she walked funny and then fell to the ground. That was a high light for us all!

In the spring we had a bus driver, Mr. Otis, who would stop the bus and let us pick buttercups. We rode a small bus with only one other family, the Zolbers. If we were late coming home our Mom wouldn't worry. She knew the buttercups were out.

I have such cherished memories of a long gone school, Reubens.

Memorable Teachers:

Miss Stone

Miss Riggers

Mrs. Anderson

Mrs. Hogaboam

Mr. Hogaboam

Mrs. Edelblute

Jerene and Pete 2012

CLASS OF 1970

Janice (Coon) Hartig

Spouse: Ron Hartig

I attended school at Reubens only 6 weeks in 1957, in the first grade. I rode the bus from the Clifford Coon (Melrose) farm to Reubens.

Special school memories during my time at Reubens:

The "bigger" kids were always kind to us "little" kids. I remember getting a penny for one of the big kids to put on the railroad track for me. I was so impressed that a train could flatten my penny. I remember Diana Hill telling me "how" to get the teacher to call on me (hand up–then down, as if I may not understand). I also remember 3 stitches in my head a result of coming off the monkey bars (?) or merry-go-round (?) dizzy and colliding with a swing.

I am grateful for the many kind folks, including the principal who made sure I had hot lunch when my ticket ran out and took me home after the "accident". Also, I am grateful for Blythe Quinn, my great aunt who kept a good eye on me from the kitchen.

Reubens school has a wonderful heritage, my short time there was memorable.

www.ingramcontent.com/pod-product-compliance
Lightning Source LLC
Chambersburg PA
CBHW080947050426
42337CB00055B/4586